Granny Buck's Dibs and Dabs:

Appalachian Traditions and Magical Ways

Catherine S. Buck

Granny Buck's Dibs and Dabs: Appalachian Traditions and Magical Ways (PUB991-23)
ISBN: 979-8-3302-2268-1
Promo Cd:
Work is categorized as Book, Poetry, Written Work, Folklore
Copyright Year: 2019
Work was submitted as Published
Year of Publication: 08/14/2019 | Nation: United States

Table of Contents

To all my family…you are the best!

Thanks to Josh B. for coming to the rescue (as always) with his computer expertise. C.A. Erickson for being my second pair of eyes and helping me set up another website, E.B. for her editing, Joel B. for his technical advice, Susan B. for reading, and Alison S. for the idea of Dark Corner. Thanks to Rick Lobs, historian and photographer for the use of the wonderful cover picture and to Rob (the voice) Leonard for his podcast.

This book is also dedicated to "the girls": Angela, Leslie and Denise, as well as Tavane and the folks at Eclectic by Nature.

Welcome to Appalachia

Covering thirteen eastern and southeastern states in the US as well as part of Canada, the Appalachian mountain's hills and its people are rich in history and discovery, a cultural melting pot with deep roots in the land. Traditional ways, stories, music and magical beliefs tell tales of these peoples' distinct cultural identity.

Scotch, German, English, Welsh or Irish stock settled into the American Appalachian backwoods beginning in the1600s. There they intermixed with the local native populations. American Indian and African-Caribbean peoples (mostly freed or runaway slaves) were their major influence. Settlers had to learn many new ways in order to survive in the rural areas with very little.

Religion was important to families living in the hills. Christian ministers that traveled through brought their religious gospel and became vital to the development of each community's educational, spiritual and social societies. Though many people who settled on the lands at that time (from the 1600s) were of Protestant faith, other cultures and religions flourished there as well, creating an interesting mix that still survives in many mountain communities today.

Generations of families developed a distinct way of thinking and believing. The use of German Powwow is still common in some mountain areas. The ability to "heal by faith," was something taught by fathers to their daughters or by mothers to their sons. Along with this special training, a person needed a strong belief in God, the use of the King James Bible, the laying on of hands and some good herbal knowledge. Powwow practitioners' used caution, fearing a talented teacher could lose their "gift" by not training someone properly or teaching the wrong person.

Hoodoo beliefs (root work, conjure and candle work) are still strong, especially towards the southern mountain foothills of Appalachia and coastal areas that include northwestern Mississippi, Alabama, Georgia and South Carolina. Slavery and the Great Migration created the Gullah people who speak a distinct English based Creole language. The mixture of West African, Native American and Christian-Catholic symbols and religious statues are commonplace in their households.

The Appalachian Cherokee and other native groups that settled in the mountains have been said to have powerful insights through shamanic journey. During states of spiritual ecstasy, stories tell of medicine people who have been able to look towards the light of the sky for answers as well as into the darkness of the underworld. Their folk traditions and stories are informative, emotional and sometimes funny. Native medicines and agricultural techniques were a huge gift to a society that had knowledge but not local familiarity.

Any type of healing was important to the community as doctors and hospitals could be many miles away. Local healers developed reputations as witches, Grannies, cunning folk, herb or root doctors, medicine people, Shamans, Pow-wow people or Hoodoo practitioners. Known for their effective healing techniques, some also had the ability to draw fire out of a burn, or remove a wart or sty from your eye, quick as a wink. They also were available to give advice on planting, and finding the best places for local farmers to dig for wells.

The expression, "Call Granny!" was a sure sign of an approaching birth. The local Granny woman kept an eye on any changes the pregnant woman may have and would prescribe the right kind of things to eat that were vitamin-enriched and teas for easy birth. When it was time for the child to be born, besides boiling water, tearing up clean rags and bringing in bags of fresh herbs used for the occasion, the granny and her helpers would also open the windows to allow fresh air into the birthing room and place an ax under the birthing bed to cut the pain. The granny herself might also inscribe symbols on the window frames to keep unhealthy things out during the labor. These women served the families in their community for hundreds of years before trained doctors became common to the region.

****

This book is, "a little bit of this and that" pertaining to Appalachian folklore traditions and magical ways. Although many techniques used by mountain families are strongly Christian based, there are many who blend Native American, African or European pagan beliefs into their lifestyles.

There are also a number of "teaching" stories sprinkled throughout the book using real techniques, ways or mountain attitudes. Found at the end of this manuscript, *Haint or Haint Not* is an intriguing mystery tale of a mountain family in the 1950s, told in the old-time storytelling tradition. It weaves together "down home" magical beliefs, along with the harsh reality of early mountain living. Sometimes a good story can tell a lot…

Reading the Signs of Nature

"Nature speaks to us. Those who stop and listen are taught much."

Granny Buck

Understanding natural signs or seasonal cycles of the weather can tell a farmer when it is the right time to plant his fields or prepare for snow or rainy days. In addition, they can help determine when many animals are safe to hunt without worms or disease in the right seasonal cycle. Much of this passed-down knowledge is available through traditional sayings. Here are some examples.

Weather Signs

"When the ditch and pond offend the nose, look out for rain and stormy blows."

- Colonial folk saying

Curious as to whether the expression above is real? Well, when there is fair weather, air pressure is high, so the scent of things (like wet, dank soil) is not as strong. On a day of low pressure, odors around you become stronger, as the change of pressure creates a stronger chance of rain.

Snow and Bad Weather

Flowers that bloom in late autumn are a sign of bad winter.

When bees build their nests high in the trees, expect a hard winter.

If corn husks are thick and tight, rough winter ahead.

If ant hills are built high in July, expect lots of snow.

When apple or onion skins are very thin,
a mild winter coming in. When apple or onion skins are thick and tough, the coming winter cold and rough.

How many snowfalls will there be in the upcoming winter? Count how many days old the moon is when the first snow begins. Three days old- three snowfalls during the winter season.

If it is a cold, cloudy day and the smoke from your fire rises, there is a chance of snow.

If spiders take down their webs, expect heavy rain.

If more than one woodpecker is living in a tree, harsh weather ahead.

An abundance of acorns in the fall, wintry weather coming.

Leaves that fall early, the fall and winter season will be mild. When leaves fall late, expect the winter to be severe.

A sign of freezing weather, pigs gather leaves and straw in their pens like a nest.

Fur on dogs is bushier. Hair on horses and cows and other livestock is thicker, too.

Squirrels' nests will be in lower branches of trees than usual.

Crows flock.

Muskrat houses and beaver's lodges are larger.

Birds gather and strip the bushes of berries faster.

If butterflies start to migrate early, there will be an early winter. You may see them gathering.

Seeing a larger than usual number of spiders and bugs looking for protection in your home or outbuildings.

Yellow jackets and hornets build heavier nests.

You see a lot more Miller moths on your light fixtures at night. They are small, thin and yellowish white to gray in color.

Rings around the Sun or Moon, rain or snow falls.

Cold August, hot July foretells a winter hard and dry.

A narrow orange band in the center of a Woolly Bear caterpillar warns of heavy snow; if the band is wide, winter will be mild. The more black and fuzzier it is, the more severe the cold.

Bushy tails on squirrels and raccoons are signs of a frigid winter.

Heavy fall crops such as pine nuts and berries.

Apples and grapes mature a lot earlier.

Dogwood and holly berries are heavy and thick.

It will rain if there is a ring around the moon at night. If you count the stars around it, it will tell you how many days before it does.

Another version: If there is a misty ring around the moon, it will rain within three days.

If you see black snakes in trees, it will rain within three days.

If onions arc larger and have more layers when they are harvested, cold weather ahead.

Leaves on the trees fall before they turn color.

The leaves of a laurel tree will curl up.

Crickets found on the hearth in early winter can be a sign a rough weather ahead.

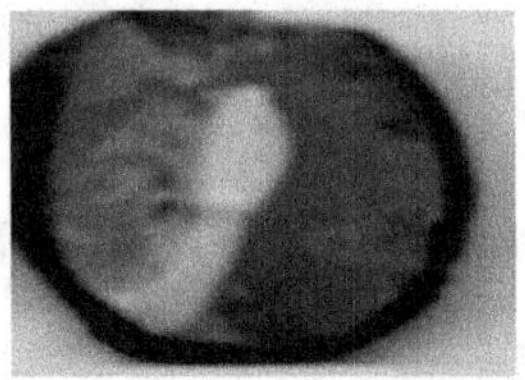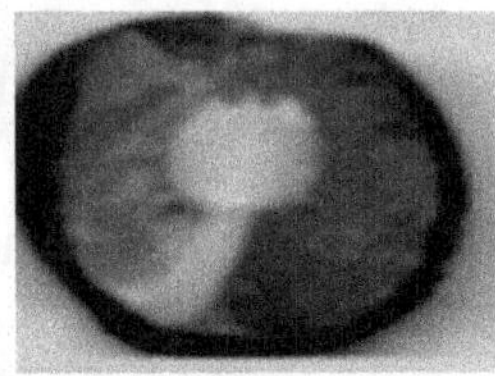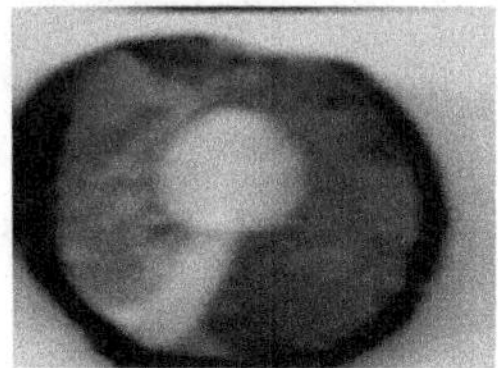

- If you cut open a Persimmon seed and see:

    A **knife shape**, icy winds

    A **fork shape**, mild winter

    A **spoon shape**, heavy, wet winter

Insects marching in a line, a sign of a hard winter.

Spiders entering the house in large numbers, a sign of freezing weather.

Thicker tree bark in the fall, a sign of a frosty winter.

Bears in the berry patch, a rough, chilly weather.

Frosts before November 23rd indicates a hard winter.

Three foggy days during the months of June and July will bring an early snow.

If it snows and the wind is blowing it in two different directions, it will be deep.

If the first snow remains on the ground for three days, another snow will come behind it.

Cold winter weather season begins if there are two or more frosts and a lot of rain. A snow storm will occur shortly after.

Signs of Rain and Mild Days

If it rains on the first day of the beginning of the full moon, it will rain, off and on, until the next quarter.

If the horns of the moon point down, it will rain within three days.

Ants will cover the hole of their anthill before it rains.

When horses and cattle stretch their necks and sniff the air, it is a sign of rain coming.

Spiders leave their webs before a storm.

Black spots on the moon means rain soon.

If dust is blowing away from the sun, it indicates dry weather; if the dust blows towards the sun, rain is on its way.

A halo or ring around the moon, you will have rain within a day.

Large numbers of fireflies flying about indicate fair weather.

When the dew on spider webs dries early in the day, the weather will be fair.

If cattle are moving towards a pasture and a bull leads them, it can be a sign of rain.

Dogs and cats get anxious before a storm.

If cows hit their tails against the fence, it will be a good weather day.

Bats flying in late evening, a good day tomorrow.

Red sky at night brings bright morning light.

Fish will come to the top of ponds before it rains.

When leaves on a tree turn up or turn over, it is a sign of rain.

Moles and chipmunks dig closer to the surface when there is clear weather.

Frogs croak louder before a rain.

When a campfire's smoke and flames rise steady, you will have a fine day ahead. If the fire and smoke are restless and close to the ground, harsh weather ahead.

White clouds are a sign of a fine day. Gray veiled clouds bring rain. Dark clouds, a storm.

Insects hide before it rains.

Birds fly closer to the ground before a storm.

Crickets stop singing before it rains.

Bees return to their hives before a storm.

Birds will nest early in the trees before rain

Signs of Earth Movement or Earthquake

Unusual sky color or cloud formations

Air is still and warm

Booming or humming noises in the air

Animals fleeing the scene

Silt in streams and rivers making water cloudy

Masses of animals or insects

Rainbow lights; sunbow

Fish beaching

Dogs howling

Streams or rivers running backwards

Headaches, or itchiness of the skin

Signs of Tornados

Dirty lemon-yellow to greenish gray sky - tornado or hail

Animals and insects go for cover

Sometimes thunder and lightning, but always hail

Everything becomes still and quiet

Wind and flying debris

Roaring sound, much like a train

***Cyclones or hurricanes spin counterclockwise in the Northern Hemisphere, and clockwise in the Southern Hemisphere.

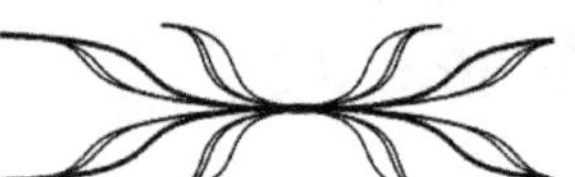

Nature shows us the direction

Are you one of those kinds of people who lose their way while walking, whether through the woods or over a mountainous area? If so, here is some helpful information that mountain people live by and have taught us. We all have within us, a sense of direction and stability. Having a fixed position gives you a sense of where you are.

Okay, so what if you are lost and you need to go west? You could: (1) walk the opposite direction from where the sun is rising (morning) in the east or forwards where the sun is setting (evening) in the west, or you could (2) push a three foot stick into the ground on a flat surface, draw a circle around the stick and watch as a shadow is cast by the sun. The end of the shadow points in a direction away from the stick. Mark that area. That is west. Then, draw a line straight across from the area you have marked. That is east.

As I have told my grandson about walking through the hills, "The minute you're lost, you're lost. Realizing this, you need to stop and center yourself. Reverse the direction you were heading and go back apiece. If that does not work, stop and try a few of these tricks. They may help you on your way to safety and home."

(Northern hemisphere only)

North

* Most moss grows on the northern side of a mountain, rock or tree. Nature does this to keep the moss from drying out from the hot sun.

* At noon, the sun is in a southward position. Walk away from the sun to begin your journey north.

* Look for the Little Dipper in the night sky. Locate the brightest star in the Dipper and walk towards it

* If you are lost in the northern continents and see a tree stump, it might help you find your way north. When you look at the tree rings, you will find one side of the rings is kind of lop-sided and closer together. That is the northern direction. The rings cluster more towards the North Pole.

* The side with the heaviest growth on a tree stump is pointing you north.

South

* Most spider webs are located on the south side of trees. Ant nests, too.

* Plants grow thicker on southern slopes. Fruits ripen faster as well.

* Snow melts first from the south side of mountains. Around here, it is most noticeable in the spring.

* When the sun is straight up in the sky (Southern direction), watch the shadows. They will begin to move in a clock-wise descend as it moves towards the west and it can help you mark time.

* If you are lost on a night when there is a crescent moon, take your finger and place it on the top point of the crescent in the sky. Move your finger downward, crossing the bottom tip of the moon to the horizon. That direction is south.

* Birds migrating, fly south.

East

  * The illuminated side of the moon can show direction as well. If the moon rises after midnight, the illuminated side will be on the east.

West

  * Large groups of animals and fish tend to breed in the west.

  * Storms normally move from west to east in North America.

  * If the moon rises before the suns sets, the illuminated side of the moon will be on the west.

Also:

>) People tend to move towards water to live. If you are lost, follow a stream or river downward to locate other people.

>) You can climb to the highest point in the area to locate any roads or towns around you.

>) Observe well while you are walking. This could lead you back to safely or keep you from wasting your time going around in circles. By marking the trail, you can be located if it is an emergency.

Folklore and Farm Wisdom

The farmer is the cultural backbone of the mountain community. In the Appalachians, large subsistent farms are few. Most people settled around large farms or a common area where they could be close to a water source and have access to food. Below are some folklore sayings of a different nature, each giving advice from the people of the past who farmed or raised livestock.

* If a person gives you seeds, roots or plants, do not thank them. If you do, they will not grow well.

* To burn wood from a tree struck by lightning is bad luck.

* Use Mullein plant as a candlewick when making candles if you do not have cotton or flax string. Farmers also used its leaves as insoles for shoes and for floor coverings. Dipped in tallow, the stalks can be used as emergency torches. Be sure to strip its leaves first. It's known as **miners' candle**.

* When harvesting apples, leave one apple on each tree to keep the devil at bay.

* When planting fruit trees, eat some sugar. The fruit from the trees will be sweeter.

* Oats and finely chopped snapdragon is given to sick chickens to eat so they can clean out their system.

* Eating ground pumpkin seed gets rid of worms.

* It is good luck to steal a piece of a plant you can grow.

* White cows are bad luck.

* Prune trees when the moon descends (darkens). The sap will be low.

* Avoid encountering a hare or a rabbit before sunrise; seeing one before then can bring unhappiness.

* Plant potatoes at the dark of night so its eyes will not see the light.

* If you find a four-leaf clover, make a wish and put it in your shoe. When the clover is gone,
  your wish will come true.

* Seeds grow better when they are planted on even days of the month.

* When eating an apple, count the number of seeds in its core; the number of your seeds will be a
  lucky number for you.

* A green Christmas could indicate a white Easter.

* Chop small pieces of southernwood in the horse's feed to rid it of worms.

* Plant corn on a new moon.

* If you step on a spider, it will bring rain.

* Burn some allspice to attract money. Cinnamon is good for that too.

* Mix wine vinegar, wine, sulfur and honey to treat wounds for infection on horses and cows.
  Good for burns, too.

* Feed your rabbits dry oatmeal to get rid of hairballs.

* Fruit picked at the new moon will store longer.

* Fruit picked on a full moon should be eaten at once as the fruit rots quickly.

* Dill will increase milk production with cows and goats.

* Gather acorns during a storm. Put on your windowsills to prevent lightning from striking the
  house.

* Marigolds are eaten by livestock as a heart treatment.

* Hollies planted around the house protect it from witchcraft and storms.

* Pole beans planted at night will grow the best crops.

* Hens lay twice as many eggs when you sprinkle garlic in their food.

* Hens lay better if you mix powdered rabbit dung with chicken feed.

* Flowers that bloom out of season are unnatural.

* Keep a goat in your milking barn if you have a cow that has aborted their calf. The goat's smell will keep the other cows from aborting.

* Tie white string across your garden to keep birds away.

* Add orange, lemon or grapefruit peels to your cows' feed. It will keep them healthy.

* Beans should be planted in the early morning, so they can produce sooner.

* If you sing in the milking shed, the milk will stop flowing.

* During the old moon (last quarter), pick apples and pears. If bruised, the bruised spots will dry up. Picking them on the new moon will cause the spots to rot.

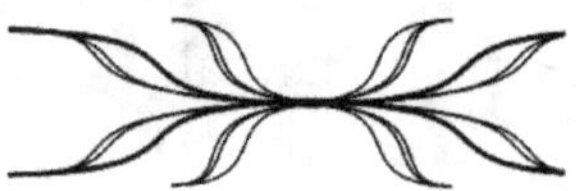

Water-Witching

Water witch – "A person who professes to have the power to sense and find underground water with a divining rod; dowser. "

* Webster's New World College Dictionary, 4th Edition. Copyright © 2010 by Houghton Mifflin Harcourt.

Moses Frawley's eyes focused forward as he walked back and forth across a patch of the farmer's property. The old man moved slowly in a series of straight lines a couple of feet apart from each other. In his hands, he holds a two-foot forked branch, cut from a willow tree.

Cradled in his palms were the limbs' ends; their wooden tips lying over the index fingers of his hands. Pulling the y-shaped branches slightly apart, the joint between the two branches arched upward in an angle and pushed outward an arm's length from his body as he moved forward.

Walking that way for about twenty minutes, he stops and reaches into his jacket pocket to pull out a folded piece of paper. Spreading it out, he looks down at the rough drawing of the sections of land he had walked over earlier that morning. He makes a mark with his pencil.

Replacing the paper in his jacket, the man proceeds to move across the back section of the field to douse the rest of the land. Forty feet into the walk, the tips of the rods suddenly seem to vibrate and start to dip downwards towards the ground. Pulling the paper out, the old man marks the place where he is standing with an X on the paper.

Pausing, he closes his eyes for a long moment and takes a deep breath. Reaching into a bag attached to his belt, the man pulls out a marker made of stiff wire topped with a small piece of red cloth. Bending down, he pushes the wire into the soil to pinpoint the area that the rods reacted to. This will go on until all the area is walked. There may be none or many Xs on his map by the end of the day. It will take a number of days or weeks of walking, mapping and studying the property until the dowser decides the right area for the well to be dug.

Named after the first "water witch", Moses (like in the bible), his mother considered the man to be blessing at birth. Their family is said to have come from a lengthy line of mountain dowsers or "water witches." His mother, Alma, was well known and sought after in the region. Before she passed away, she taught the craft to her son.

The week before, Moses met the man at his farm just before dawn. Together, they looked at the map and deed of the farmer's property while they had their breakfast. After the meal, the old man thanked his host, pulled out a piece of paper and pencil from his pocket, and began to roughly sketch a copy of the property and its boundaries.

In the process of "water-witchin", Moses then asks if any other wells have been dug or drilled on the property, or if there are any other streams, creeks or marshy areas. He also asks about any active pastureland or any areas on which pesticides were used in the past year or two. They also discuss the weather patterns that had occurred around there in the past few years. As the sun rises, they leave the farmhouse and walk the land.

Types of Dowsing Rods

1. Y-shaped forked sticks from trees such as willow, peach or witch hazel.

2. You can also use a coat hanger cut into two pieces, copper wire rods, a Bobber or a pendulum for dowsing.

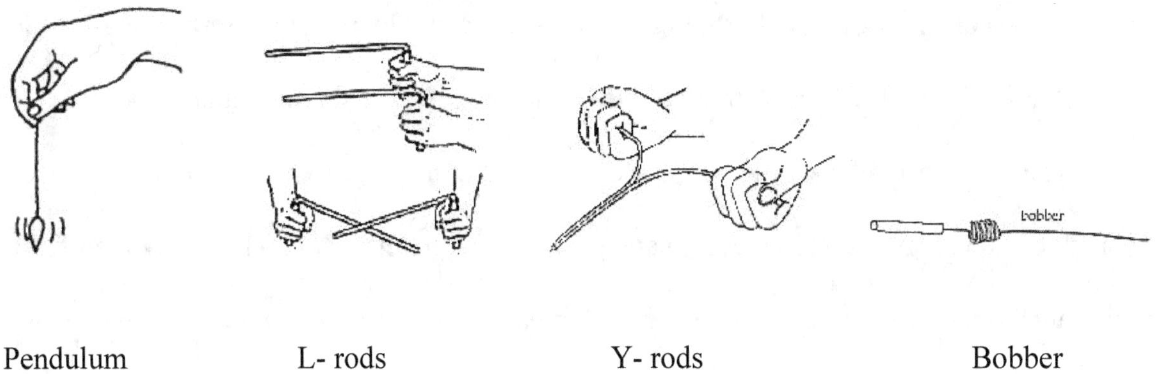

| Pendulum | L- rods | Y- rods | Bobber |

How to Dowse

1. If you use Y-rods or L-rods, remember that they should be 2 feet on each side and equal in length.

2. Keep them an arm's length, away from the body. Focus on what you are dowsing for. If it is water, picture in your mind water moving under the ground as you walk.

3. Walk in a straight line; don't hold the rods tightly; balance them on tops of your fingers, allowing them to have movement. Keep the butt of the rods in the palms of your hands.

4. Practice walking back and forth until you feel you are attuning yourself to your dowsing tools and to the area you are working with. Make yourself aware of any minor changes or movements of the rod as you work.

5. If water is detected, you should be able to feel the rods rotate or pull downward in your palms. The rods will usually cross over each other. Y-shaped wooden rods will pull down.

Signs for spotting areas for potential wells:

1. **Natural groundwater commonly trickles down mountain slopes and if not used, ends up in rivers, streams or marshes.** One of the first things a water witch or dowser does is to mark the areas of farmland known to have a history of moisture or water outflow on his working map.

2. **Clumps of vegetation or trees that stay green, even during drought, usually have groundwater underneath.** A well-trained eye would also watch for particular types of trees, shrubs or plants. River birch, willow, pin oak or wild persimmons grow well around moist areas. Bottlebrush buckeye, hollies and viburnum are a few shrubs that need a good access to moist soil. Smaller plants to look for are ferns, Solomon seal, meadow rue, iris, astilbe, bleeding hearts, wild cowslips or trillium.

3. **Look for moisture under rocks and boulders.**

4. **After it rains, watch for the sign of earthworms coming to the surface, especially around areas where it is marked on your map as a possible well.** A lot of moisture in the ground brings the earthworms to the surface.

5. **Look around for termite mounds.** The insects usually will not mound unless there is a water source nearby.

6. **Animal tracks on the ground or birds' nests in the trees means there is a water source in the area.**

7. **Look for areas with porous rock, such as limestone, sandstone, chalk, pumice or lava rock, as they are known to collect water.**

Note: An abundant amount of surface ground water is preferred for a good well. Check to make sure there are no problems with saltiness or methane. If a well is dug too deep, or the seasonal water table is down, there could be problems.

Wildcrafting

Wildcraft or Foraging - The practice of harvesting plants from their natural areas for the use of medicine or food.

Fall Harvest and the Root Digger

Molly Buck had walked the land all during the past spring and summer, mostly observing and writing down information. Her notepad was full of things relating to plant sites for harvesting. The little book, along with her wildcrafting tools were stored in her grandson David's old school bag. He had given it to her a couple of years ago because his mother had bought him another one that was a little fancier. Molly was glad to have it. She could not bear to waste anything that had such a great purpose. It had enough pockets to put all the things she needed, separate from each other and safe. She could even strap it on her back.

It was a good thirty-minute walk up the side of the ridge on Baker Mountain and she didn't want to forget anything. The darkness outside was starting to turn gray. It will be sun-up soon and even though it was now September, she wanted to be back before twelve noon; never know who may come by for dinner. David was out of school at 2:30 and he said he was going to get the bus to drop him nearby. Chuckling, she thought, "Better take out two bags of peaches from the freezer to thaw out for dinner. David can eat one just by himself."

Her daughter Louise had brought her a bushel basket of the fruit last summer and she peeled, sliced and laid up the bags in the freezer with a tablespoon of sugar added to each one. Unthawed and cold, they were wonderful anytime.

Drinking her last sip of coffee, she looked on the table to make sure she had everything she needed before she set out. Here is what was laid out on the table:

A medium sized woven basket

Digging stick / walking stick - the one with an iron tip

Floppy hat

Pack of hand wipes

Lightweight jacket with pockets

Compass

5 paper luncheon bags

One dozen large size freezer bags

One dozen small size freezer bags

A sheet of labels (A spool of paper tape works well, too.)

Pair of gardening gloves

Her wildcrafting notebook and two sharpened pencils

Scissors

Fold out knife

Pruning shears

Small hand hatchet with case

Small fold-up hand shovel

Three bottles of water

Two boiled eggs and an apple

Small baggy filled with baking soda

Insect repellent

Packing her bag, she left a few items out to carry either in her jacket pockets or in her jeans. Before she left, she took a good look (one more time) at the clothing she was wearing. She wore a long-sleeved cotton t-shirt, jeans, heavy socks and a pair of grungy, thick-leathered farm boots that had seen many a day. She had her jeans tucked into her boots to protect her legs from snake or insect bites. Then, she checked to make sure her small wallet was in her back pocket. Donning her coat, she placed her gloves and hand wipes in her right pocket and her notebook, one pencil and the compass in the left. She had put a note on her table the night before, explaining why she was out and where. Louise knew where her mother was going this morning, too.

Chuckling, she thought, "I would have never left notes and such, but at my age, you can't be too cautious; the stooping and digging can tucker a body out. It's hot work, too." She rubbed her hand across her face and pulled a strand of hair behind her ear.

Zipping up her pack, she put her jacket on and grabbed her willow basket and walking stick as she headed out the door.

It was a beautiful morning. The gold and shimmering pink of the sky bled down into the forest of trees around her. The sun began to peek over the mountain's ridge and you could see the dragon's breath (fog) curling up around the sides of the hills nearby. The woods were still green, but glancing across the treetops, she could see the bits of brown, yellow or orange autumn leaves. Walking up the path with her stick in hand, she paused and took a satisfied breath. Going forward at her own pace, she gradually became a small figure moving up the trail heading towards her destination.

She had come early to forage the ridge. It was only the second day of September, but she wanted to check and make sure no one else had been digging in the same patches and if so, whether anything was still there for her to use. Though there were many things to gather and eat in the wild areas around her, the old woman had decided not to gather too many different things. This trip was for her to stockpile the roots and herbs she needed to make her medicines for winter. A bunch of people will be knocking on her door for a healing then. Why, her cough medicines were some of the best in the county!

Her grandson David once asked her how she was able to recognize so much when it came to herbs. She told him that she learned from her pa and her pa learned from his ma. Her daddy was good at finding all kinds of things. He knew a lot about the use of local plants. He also made boxes and baskets, mostly out of the bark of water birch trees, and enjoyed gathering mushrooms. They say he had a hidden ginseng patch, but he never told anyone its location before he died. The old woman told her grandson that in the spring, he could go up into the hills with her to harvest roots and leaves. "David's learning a little older than me," she thought. "He is eleven now; by the time he's thirteen, he should be able to work with the family recipes and make things for healing. Her grandson came from a long line of cunning folk and he understood that he had to uphold his family's tradition."

As she walked, her mind went back to the beginning of her first lessons. What were some of the first things she learned as a child about hunting and collecting wild plants? It has been on her mind a lot recently. Her Pa started taking her out at age eight, and right off, he told her that she needed to recognize the poisonous plants first before anything. The ones you shouldn't eat. The ones you shouldn't even touch, or you could get sick and possibly die. If you have to collect them, you need to wear gloves. Another thing he cautioned me about was that I should not harvest any herbs where there has been pesticide use and to stay away from roads in my foraging, as the plants around the roads will absorb exhaust from vehicles.

That same year, he taught her how to read the weather signs. He also showed her ways to obtain water if she couldn't find any. Sometimes, he would take her out on a picnic and afterwards show her the best places where birds make their nests and where certain animals made their dens.

She was ten years old when her Pa told her a way to "tell the bees" if the beekeeper died. Then he looked down at her for a moment, all quiet-like, and said, "Molly, you may have to do it one day."

And she did, in later years...she knocked on three of their bee hives and announced to them that her husband Owen had died.

It was in October when she turned thirteen that Molly and her father came upon a lightning-struck mulberry tree. They'd had a storm a week or so back and one side of the tree was all burned and black from the lightening. Taking his knife, her Pa cut some strips from the tree and put them in his birch box that he always carried. He knew her Mam was beginning to teach her about oils and distilling and she was doing well with it. He said that lightning-struck wood is a powerful, spiritual medicine. He knew her mother would be happy that he had found it.

Almost there. Molly spotted a Chicken of the Woods mushroom growing on the side of a rotted oak tree as she was walking by. The golden colored mushroom was good eating and this one was a fairly good size. She sliced it off the bark with her knife and put it into her basket. She'll need to cut it in half in order to pack it into the largest freezer bags she brought with her. Smiling, she mumbled to herself, "I'm after burdock root today, but if I run across somethin' special, I'm not gonna pass it up. Waste not, want not."

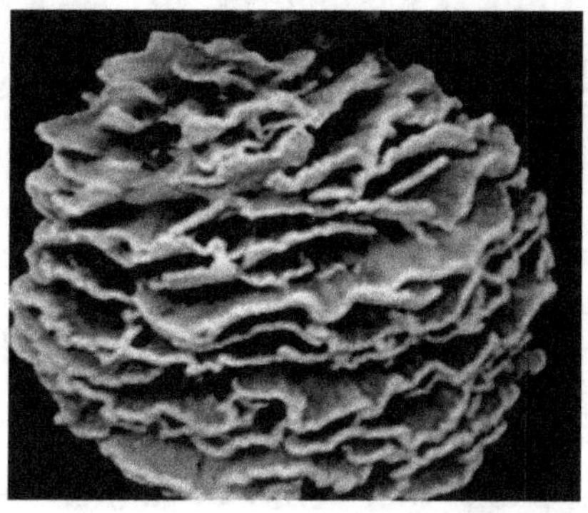

She arrived at the field and looked around. Doesn't look like it had any visitors. Taking the backpack off, she leans over and puts her digging stick next to the rock she sits down on. She then puts her basket on the ground, takes out her gloves from her pocket and removes her fold-out shovel and some big freezer bags from the back of the pack. Two of the bags she labeled and dated on the front. Then, she put a star design on the label with her pencil. The star represented the location she got it from. She records the find in her notebook, cuts her special find in half, and places a piece of the mushroom in each bag. She then slides the bags into her basket.

The burdock patch was growing on the side of the field. She had to step into the weeds to get to the cluster of plants she wanted. Burrs from the older plants stuck to her jeans as she walked through. Looking around, she thought: "Don't want any second year plants with rotted roots, though I can't say they don't have any use." Reaching over, she cut off a couple clusters of the burrs and four of the flower tops from the tall, older plants and put them in some of the smaller freezer bags.

Molly was looking for young plants; the ones with just leaves that did not have stalks or burrs. She found two good size ones in a piece of compacted soil. Even with the soil being that way, she realized she was glad she came up there today. She knew the fall roots were better for medicine and were normally larger. The two plant clusters she found should have some nice, big roots for simples (medicine).

She broke the top of the ground next to them with her digging stick, but she realized quickly that her shovel would work better and picked it up off the ground. She had to dig deep around the plants to break the soil loose. Roots on a burdock were sometimes three feet long, so she had her work cut out for her. Once she dug around them, she would have to pull them straight up in order to get them out of the ground.

Roots

About an hour later, it was done. She had two nice clusters of roots on the ground in front of her. She cut off the tops and placed the large, younger leaves in three of the big freezer bags to take home as well. Then she stopped for a few minutes to rest and eat. She took two of the bottles of water out of her pack, leaving the extra one just in case she needed it. One she drank with her lunch and the other she opened to rinse the roots clean. Taking out her old towel, she wiped the roots and then pulled her hatchet out of its case. Laying the roots in the grass, she chopped them into strips to dry better. She collected enough to fill up three large freezer bags, which she then labeled and packed into the basket. The roots will need to be soaked when they get home in a tub of water to get out the "earthy" taste.

Taking a glove full of burrs, she started scraping them onto the dirt she was replacing in the holes she dug. Hopefully, when she came back in the spring, new plants would already be started. When she finished, she packed up her things and started for home.

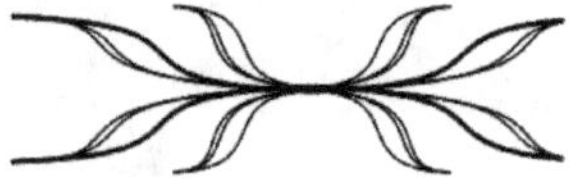

How to Make Root Medicines
"The land gives us many good things. Its roots help us to heal."

Making a root tincture is easy. Wash the roots and dry them before cutting. Chop into small pieces. Take note that fresh roots shrink if not used quickly. Take one ounce of the chopped root per two ounces of alcohol. Use a higher proof alcohol as it acts as a preservative. 100 proof grain alcohol is best.

You will need to weigh the empty jar first. Add the measured alcohol to the roots and weigh again. Subtract weight of the jar to get the true weight value of the mixture. Depending on how much you are making, you need to store it in a jar with a screw top lid. Replace the lid back on the jar and place in a dark, cool place. Shake or mix it every day for eight weeks. Any time after that period, you can press and pour the concentrated root tincture out into smaller containers.

Roots to Collect for Fall Harvest

Angelica - Best collected in the first year of growth. The plant peaks in autumn.

Bistort - Both root and the rootstock are collected and used.

Black Cohosh - After the fruits have ripened in autumn, the root and rootstock are collected.

Black Haw - Dig up the root and scrape off the outer bark.

Blood Root - Make sure the leaves at the top of the plant have died out and dried up before harvesting the rootstock.

Blue Cohosh - Harvest root and rootstock in the fall.

Blue Flag – Both root and rootstalk can be used.

Burdock - From mid-September to October is the best time to collect these. Harvest root and rootstock.

Calamus - Harvest root and rootstock from September to October.

Comfrey – Wait until late fall or winter to harvest the root. Leaves are collected in spring.

Couchgrass - Early autumn is the best time to harvest rootstalk.

Echinacea - Two to three year old plants are harvested in the fall.

Elecampane - Mid-September to October is the best time to dig this rootstock.

False Unicorn Root - Root and rootstalk are gathered in autumn.

Garlic - September is the time to harvest garlic. Take from the ground when the leaves start to die.

Ginger - Another fall harvested root. Collect when leaves begin to die.

Ginseng - Berries are produced in the fifth year. These roots and seeds will be mature enough to harvest when the berries turn dark red.

Goldenseal - Only harvest if the plants are four to five years old. Harvest root when top dies down.

Gravel Root - Collect root and rootstock after flowers no longer bloom.

Horseradish - Harvest root from first freeze up to early spring.

Licorice - Harvesting root should take place on or after the third year.

Marshmallow - Harvest only the root of four year old or older plants in the fall.

Poke Root - Late fall is the best time for harvest after the top plant dies off. Caution: Wear gloves. Poisoning can occur from dermal absorption.

Sassafras Root - Harvest rook in November.

Skunk Cabbage - Harvest root and rootstock in the fall.

Snake Root - Root and root bark collected in the autumn.

Soapwort - Collect root from mid-September through October.

Valerian - The best time to harvest this root is in October.

Wild Indigo – Harvest the root after last flowering of the season.

Yellow Dock – Roots harvested from August through October.

Roots to Collect for Spring Harvest

** **Note:** Many of the fall roots listed above are harvested in the spring as well. **

Cattail – Harvest roots, shoots and pollen late spring or early summer.

Dandelion – Flowers, leaves or roots are collected in the spring or fall.

Evening Primrose – Biennial – It flowers in its second year. Harvest first year root before any flowers appear.

Jerusalem Artichoke – **Sunchokes or Earthapples** are their folk names. Gather late fall or early winter.

Nettle Root – Best time to harvest the root is late fall to early spring.

Note: Mushrooms are harvested wild in all seasons. Start watching for them to reappear after the last frost.

* * * * * * *

Why do Plants and Trees have Folk Names?

Revered by man for thousands of years, plants, shrubs and trees have become major symbols of the power of nature. Sprouting from the earth, their life cycles of growth, decay and rebirth have become part of many tales and legends. Descriptive meanings in folklore give them a purpose name rather than a scientific one.

These folk names can describe their color, scent, look or shape; whether they have thorns, are toxic or have healing properties. Natural herbs are still being tested both for their safety as well as for medical properties.

Folk Names of Herbs

Common Name	Folk Name
Aconite: Napellus	Monkshood, Blue Rocket, Friar's Cap, Soldier's Cap, Helmet Flower, Hecate, Turk's Cap
Aconite: Lycoctonum	Wolfsbane, Wolf Killer plant, Mousebane, Leopard's Bane
Adders Tongue	Fawn Lily, Trout Lily, Dog's-tooth Violet, Adders Fork
Adders Tongue Fern	Snake Tongue, Cock's-comb, Drago Tongue
Agaric, Fly	Death Angel Deadly Amanita, Death Cap, Fly Killer, Magic Mushroom, Redcap
Agrimony	Church Steeples, Burr Marigold Garclive, Fairy's Wand, Cockleburr

Common Name	Folk Name
Agropyrum	Dog Grass, Twitch, Quick Grass, Quitch Grass
Alder	Owler, Fairy Tree, King of the Forest
Amaranth	Red Cockscomb, Cockscomb and Love Lies Bleeding
American Valerian	Ram's Head, Setwall and All-Heal
Angelica	Archangel, Angel Food, Masterwort, Ground Ash, Holy Ghost Root
Anthemis cotula	Mayweed, stinking Chamomile, Mather, Dog or hog's-fennel, Dog-finkle, Dog-daisy, Pig-sty-daisy, Chigger-weed
Asafetida	Angedan, Devil's Dung, Stinking Gum
Ash	Goat's Foot, Hoop Ash, Nion, Spear Tree, Toothache Tree, Yellow Wood
Aster	Starworts, Michaelmas Daisies or Frost Flowers
Avens	Hare's Foot or Star of the Earth, Herb Bennet, Colewort and St. Benedict's Herb
Bachelor's Buttons	Devil's flower, Bluet, Blue Bottle, Devil's Flower, Hurtlesickle, Red Campion

Common Name	Folk Name
Bald Cypress	Graybeard of the Swamp, Swamp Cypress
Bear's Breeches	Blood from a Shoulder, Sea Dock, Bearsfoot, or Oyster Plant
Belladonna	Witches Berry, Death Herb, Deadly Nightshade, Divale, Death Cherries, Beautiful Death, Dwale, Dwaleberry, Banewort, Devil's Berries, Naughty Man's Cherries, Devil's Herb, Great Morel
Betony	Bishop's Wort Lamb's Ears, Common Hedgenettle, Betony, Wood Betony, Bishopwort, Purple Betony
Birch	Lady of the Woods, Birce, Bierce, Bog Birch, Swamp Birth
Bistort	Dragon Wort, Meadow Bistort, Snakeweed, Common Bistort, Snake-root and Easter-ledges
Blackberry	Scaldhead, Black Caps, Brambleberries
Black Cohosh	Black Snakeroot, Rattletop, Rattleroot, Rattleweed, Bugbane and Macrotys
Black Haw	King's Crown, Silver Bells, Stag Bush, Snowball Tree, Cramp Bark, Rose Elder, Red Elder or May Rose
Black Spleenwort	Black Maidenhair, Mountain Shield Fern, Holly Fern, Marsh Fern and Lady Fern
Bloodroot	Indian Paint, Red Root, Bloodwort, Red Puccoon Root, Pauson, Tetterwort, Sweet Slumber and Snakebite

Common Name	Folk Name
Blue Bells	Ring-of-Bells, Harebell, Wild Hyacinth, Wood Bell, Fairy Flower and Bell Bottle.
Bluets	Innocence, Loggerheads, Centaury, Centory, Starthistles and Knapweed
Borage	Burrage, Common Bugloss, Tailwort, Beebread and Star Flower
Brier Hips	Witch's Brier, Briar Rose, Sweet Briar, Dog Rose, Hip Fruit, Wild Brier and Eglantine
Buckthorn	Black Dogwood, Bone of an Ibis, Alder Buckthorn, Alder Dogwood, Arrowwood, Berry-alder, Bird Cherry, Black Alder Dogwood and Black Alder Tree
Bugle Weed	Wolf's Foot, St. Lawrence Plant, Carpetweed, Bugle, Blue Bugle, Carpet Bugleweed
Burdock	Cockle Buttons, Love Leaves, Personata, Happy Major, Clot-Bur, Beggar's Buttons, Thorny Burr, Major and Fox's Clote
Bulbous Buttercup	Frog's Foot, Crazyweed, St. Anthony's Turnip, Crow's Foot, and Wood Anemone
Buttercup	Toe of Frog, Common Water Crowfoot, Swamp Buttercup, Blister Plant, Pond Crowfoot
Calamus	Dragon's Blood, Beewort, Bitter Pepper Root, Calamus Root, Flag Root and Mongolian Poison
Calendula	Bride of the Sun, Pot Marigold, Ruddles, Common Marigold and Scotch Marigold

Common Name	Folk Name
Carob	John's Bread, Locust, The Black Gold of Cyprus
Carrot	Bird's Nest, Bee's-nest, Bird's-nest, Bird's-nest Root, Carotte (French), Carrot, Common Carrot, Crow's-nest, Daucon, Dawke, Devil's-plague, Fiddle, Gallicam
Cedar	Tree of Life, Arbor Vitae, Cedar of Lebanon, Blood of Kronos
Celandine	Swallowwort, Felonwort, Wartweed, Sightwort, Kenningwart, Tetterwort, Killwort, Devil's Milk
Chamomile	Blood of Hestia, Dog-elder, Dog's-mercury, Ground Apple, Whig plant, Dog's-chamomile, Dog-rose, Dog's Tail Plant
Chickweed	Starweed, Hen's Inheritance, Long-Leaved Stitchwort, Fever Plant
Chicory	Old Man's Beard, Ragged Sailors, Country-folk, Beggar's staff, Jacob's Rod, Long-wort, Hare's Beard, Aaron's Rod
Cinquefoil	Five Fingers, Five Leaf Grass, Hornwort, Hare's-tail, Silver Weed, Soldier's Wound Wort
Clary Sage	Clear eye, Eyebright, Salvia
Clover	Semen of Ares, Trefoil, Honey-suckles, and Common White Clover
Club Moss	Stag's Horn, Wolf's Claw, Tree-moss, Fox-feet, Buck-grass, Creeping Bur, Forks and Knives, Buck-grass, Creeping Bur, Forks and Knives

Common Name	Folk Name
Cockhold	Beggar's Tick, Spanish Needles, Devil's Pitchfolk
Coltsfoot	Bull's Foot or Horse's Hoof, Horsefoot, Dovedock, Sowfoot, Colt-herb, Hoofs, Cleats, Ass's-foot, Foalfoot, Foalswort, Ginger, Clayweed
Comfrey	Ear of an Ass, Soapwort, Boneset, Knitbone, Yalluc, Slippery Root, Gum Plant, Consound Bruisewort and Wallwort
Cowslip	Fairy Cup, Herb Peter, Keys-of-heaven, Paigle, Palsywort, Peter's Keys, St Peter's Keys
Dandelion	Priest's Crown or Lion's Tooth, Danewort, Daneweed, Dane's Blood, Piss-abed and Wet-a-bed
Daisy	Eye of the Day, Soapwort, Day's Eye, Dwarf Flax, Purging Flax, Líon Beag, Thunder Daisy and Moon Daisy
Datura	Devil's Apple, Witch's Thimble, Thorn, Crazy Plant, Devil's Weed, Yerba del Diablo
Dill	Semen of Hermes, Dulldill, Dilly, Garden Dill, Chebbit, Sowa, Keper, Hulwa, and Buzzalchippet
Dill Seed	Hairs of a Baboon, Meetin' Seed, Meeting House Seeds and Aneton
Dodder	Devil's Guts, Witch's Hair, Beggarweed, Hellweed, Strangle Tare, Scaldweed
Dogstooth Violet	Adders Tongue, Lungwort Stitch Wort, Frankincense Comfrey, Auricula, Stinking Hellebore, Snail Plant, Adam and Eve

Common Name	Folk Name
Echinacea	Black Sampson, Purple Daisy, Hedgehog Coneflower, and Sampson Root
Elecampane	Elf Wort, Elf-dock, Eolone, Horseheal, Scabwort, and Wild Sunflower
Eyebright	Rock Rue, Eyes, Mayflower, Wild Pink, Wild Lily, Toad- flax, Ragged Robin, None-so-pretty, Lady's-fingers and Four-o'clocks
Fenugreek	Bird's Foot, Greek Hay, Alholva, Greek Clover, Greek Hayseed
Fern	Skin of a man, Bear Paw, Ramsons, Rock Fern, Venus Hair
Figwort	Crowdy Kit, Heal All, Knotty-Rooted Figwort, Kernelwort, Carpenter's Square
False Unicorn	Unicorn Horn, Alétris, Blazing Star, Fairy Wand, Starwort
Fleabane	Colt's Tail, Semen of Hephaistos, Dogbane, Leopard's Bane, Henbane
Foxglove	Bloody Fingers, Witch's Gloves, Witches' Thimbles, Fairy Fingers, Witch's Bells, Witches' Hats
Fumitory	Earth Smoke, Wax Dolls, Beggary, Vapor, Scabweed, Fumus
Garlic	Stink Weed, Poor Man's Treacle, Stinking Rose, Ajo, and Garlicke

Common Name	Folk Name
Geranium	Crow's Foot, Dove's Foot, Woodland Geranium, Spotted Cranesbill and Shameface
Ginseng	True Ginseng, Five Fingers, Tartar Root, Red Berry, Man's Health, Ren Shen, Man Root, Finger Root and Wonder of the World
Goldenrod	Aaron's rod, Blue Mountain Tea, Goldruthe, Gonea Tea, Solidago, Wound Weed, Bohea Tea and Woundwort
Goldenseal	Yellow Paint Root, Eye Root, Indian Dye, Eye Balm, Yellow Root, Eye root, Ground Raspberry, Orangeroot and Yellow Puccoon
Goosegrass	Cleavers, Clivers, Catchweed, Sticky Willy, Sticky Willow, Robin~run~the~hedge, Stickyweed, Velcro Weed, Grip Grass, Clabber Grass, Coachweed, Click, Everlasting Friendship
Gorse	Broom, Frey, Furze, Gorst, Goss, Prickly Broom, Ruffett, Whin, Thorny Broom, Prickly Broom
Gravelroot	Kidney Root, Trumpet Weed, Purple or Tall Boneset, Gravelweed, Jopi Weed, Queen of the Meadow Root, Joe-Pye Weed, Hempweed
Ground Ivy	Cat's Foot, Gill-over-the-ground, Creeping Charlie, Alehoof, Tunhoof, Catsfoot, Field Balm, and Run-away-robin, Haymaids, Hedgemaids, Hove and Lizzy-run-up-the-hedge
Hawk Weed	Mouse's Ear, King Devil, Yellow Hawkweed, Bouquet Rouge, Devil's Paintbrush, Grimm the Collier, Felon Herb, Mouse Bloodwort and Yellow Devil
Hart's Tongue Fern	Cow's Tongue, Deer Tongue, God's Hair, Horse's Tongue, Hind's Tongue
Hawthorn	Tree of Chastity, Hagthorn, Bread and Cheese Tree, May Tree, May, Whitethorn, Hagthorn, Quickthorn, Ladies' Meat, May Bush

Common Name	Folk Name
Heliotrope	Cherry Pie, Tumsole, Velvetleaf Soldierbush, Tree Heliotrope, Veloutier, Octopus Bush
Hemlock	Carrot Fern, Devil's Bread, Devil's Porridge, Poison Parsley, Spotted Corobane, Sporred Hemlock
Hemp	Agrimony, St. John's Herb (not Wort), Holy Rope, Thoroughwort, Justice Weed, Yankeeweed, Dog- Fennel
Hibiscus	Jamaica Sorrel, Karkade, Karkadi, Red Sorrel, Red Tea, Shoeflower, China Tea
Holly	Christ's Thorn, Holy Tree, Hulver, Holme, Holme Chase, and Bat Wings
Honeysuckle	Irish Vine, Woodbine, Fairy Trumpets, Honeybind, Goat's Leaf, Trumpet Flowers and Sweet Suckle
Horehound	Eye of the Star, Bull's Blood, Seed of Horus, Burning Bush and False Dittany
Horsetail	Scouring Rush, Bottle Brush and Shave Grass, Paddock Pipes, and Horsetail Rush
Hound's Tongue	Tongue of Dog, Dog's Tongue, Gypsy Flower, Gypsyflower, and Rats and Mice
House Leek	Thunder Plant, From the Foot, Liveforever, St. Patrick's Cabbage, Thunder Plant, Common Houseleek, Hen and Chickens, Old Man, Roof Houseleek, Bullock's Beard, Bullock's Eye, Devil's Beard, Earwort, Fuet, Healing Blade, Homewort, Imbroke, Jove's Beard, Jupiter's Beard, Jupiter's Eye, Poor Jan's Leaf
Hydrangea	Seven Barks, Seven Bark Powers, Pom-pom, Water Vessel and Snow Plant

Common Name	Folk Name
Indian Pipe	Corpse Plant, Fairy Smoke, Eyebright, Indian-pipe, One-flower, Ghost Flower
Inkberry	American Cancer, American nightshade, American Spinach, Bear's Grape, Cancer-root, Coakum, Garget, Inkweed, Pigeonberry, Poke, Pokeweed, Red-ink Plant, Skoke Berry, Virginia Poke, Crow Berry, Pokeroot, Pokeberry
Jasmine	White Poison Vine, Sweet Jasmine, Yasmyn, Jessamyn and Moonlight on the Grove
Knotweed	Fleece Flower, Sparrow's Tongue, Japanese Bamboo, Mexican Bamboo and Bombascus
Lady's Bedstraw	Yellow Bedstraw, Cheese Rennet, Maidenhair, Our Lady's Bedstraw, A Little Dandy, Petty Mugger
Lady's Mantle	Frauenmantle, Bear's Foot, Lion's Hook, Nine Hooks, Ladies Cloak, Breakstone, Woman's Best Friend, Pied-de-Lion
Larkspur	Elijah's Chariot, Lark's claw, Lark's Heel, Low Larkspur, Little Larkspur and Montane Larkspur
Laurel	Bay, Common Cherry Laurel, Baie, Bay Tree, Daphne, Grecian Laurel, Sweet Bay, Spoonwood
Lavender	Elf Leaf, Spike, Old English Lavender, True Lavender and Nard
Lemon Balm	Heart's Desire, Bee Balm, Dropsy Plant, Balm, Thé de France, Balm Mint, Heart's Delight, Melissa, and Elixir of Life
Lettuce (Wild)	Sleepwort, Blood of a Titan, Wild Lettuce, Compass Plant, Wild Opium, Horse Thistle, Bitter Lettuce, Prickly Lettuce

Common Name	Folk Name
Liatris	Blazing Star, Spire, Spike, Gayfeather, Purple Poker, Kansas Gay, Feather, Button Snakeroot
Licorice	Root, Sweet Root, Black Sugar, Sweetwood, Regliss, Spanish Licorice, Russian Licorice, Russian Licorice
Lily of the Valley	May Lily, May Bells, Our Lady's Tears, Mary's Tears, May Lily, Park Lily, May Blossom, Ladder to Heaven, Jacob's Tears and May Bell
Lovage	Love Parsley, Cornish Lovage, Maggi Plant, Smellage, Cajoler's Weed and Old English Lovage
Lupine	Blood from a Head, Dewcup, Old Maid's Bonnet, Blue Pea, Wild Bean, Sundial, Wild Pea
Magnolia	Swamp Sassafras, Blue Magnolia, Cucumber Tree, Chinese Magnolia, Sweet Bay Magnolia
Mallow	Cheeses, Schloss Tea, Mallards, French Hollyhocks, Moe the Enforcer
Mandrake	Wild Lemon, May Apple, Hog Apple, Duck's Foot and Gallows' Root
Marjoram	Greek Oregano, Winter Marjoram, Knotted Marjoram, Sweet Marjoram, Joy of the Mountain
Marigold	Herb of the Sun, Mary's Gold, American Marigold, African Marigold and Aztec Marigold African
Milk Thistle	Thistle, Variegated Thistle, St Mary's Milk Thistle, Marian Thistle, Lady's Thistle, Holy Thistle, Blessed Milk Thistle, Mary's Thistle

Common Name	Folk Name
Mistletoe	Golden Bough, All Heal, Birdlime, Thuderbesem, Devil's Fuge, Holy Wood, Ligname, Sacta Crucis, Mistle, Thuderbesem, Witches' Broom, Wood of the Cross, Kissing Bough
Morning Glory	Flying Saucer, Devil's Vine, Hedge Lily, Bindweed, Heavenly Blue
Motherwort	Lion's Tail, Heartwort, Melissa, Lion's Ear
Moss (Common)	Marsh Bryum, Bat's Wool, Carrageen
Mugwort	St. John's Herb, Tarragon, Witch's Herb, Old Man, Felon Herb, Moxa Herb, Mothwort
Mulberry Sap	Blood of a Goose, Heart Poison
Mullein	Corpse Candles, Beggar's Blanket, Witches' Candle, Quaker Rouge, Candlewick Plant, Donkey's Ears, Velvet Plant, Felt-Wort
Mustard	Field mustard, Rape Mustard, Cole Seed, Jack by the Hedge and Burning Must
Nettles	Burn Hazel, Stinging Nettle, Wild Spinach, Bee Sting Nettle, Devil's Leaf, Sting Weed, Hidgy-pidgy, Hoky-poky
Nutmeg	Qoust, Mace, Wohpala, Macis
Oak	Jove's Nuts, Juglans, Doire, Tanner's Bark

Common Name	Folk Name
Oregano	Wild Marjoram, Rigani, Bastard Marjoram, Joy of the Mountain
Pansy	Love in Idleness, Heart's Ease, Tickle my Fancy
Parsley	Devil's Oatmeal, Turnip-rooted Parsley, Hamburg Parsley
Partridge Berry	Boxberry, Squaw Vine, Lingonberry, Teaberry, Checkerberry, Mountain Tea
Passion Flower	Wild Water Lemon, Love-in-a-mist, May-pop, Grandilla, Maracoc, Passion Vine, Apricot Vine
Pennyroyal	Pudding Grass, Run-by-the-Ground, Lurk-in-the-Ditch, Organ Tea, European Pennyroyal
Peppermint	Peppery, Lammint and Brandy Mint, Balm Mint, Lamb Mint
Periwinkle	Devil's Eye, Blue Buttons, Sorcerer's Violet, Fairy Paintbrush, Gwean
Poppy	Blind Eyes, Cup of Sunlight, Corn Rose, Field Poppy, Headache, Headwark
Plantain	White Man's Footprint, Soldier's Herb, Cart Track Plant, Mother of Herbs, Dooryard Plant, Waybread, Englishman's Foot, Fleawort, Ribwort
Portulaca	Garden Purslane, Pussley, Red Root, Pig Weed, Breeze Through Rock

Common Name	Folk Name
Queen Anne's Lace	Large Bullwort, Bird's-Nest, Devil's-Plague, Bee's Nest Plant, Bishop's Flower, False Queen Anne's Lace, Queen of Africa, Wild Carrot
Ragwort	Fairies' Horses, Ragweed, Common Ragwort, Stinking Willie, Tansy Ragwort, Benweed, St. James-wort, Stinking Nanny, Staggerwort, Dog Standard, Cankerwort, Stammerwort
Red Clover	Purple Clover, Cleaver Grass, Cow Grass, Marl Grass, Trefoil, Wild Clover, Beebread, Clovone, Cow Clover, Meadow Clover Trefoil, Honey Stalks
Red Raspberry	Bramble of Mount Ida, European Red Raspberry, Hindberry, Raspis, Bramble Bush of Ida
Rosemary	Old Man, Incensier, Sea Dew, Rosmarine, Rosemarie, Dew of the Sea, Ros Maris
Rowan	Delight of the Eye, Mountain Ash, Quickbane, Ran Tree, Roden-Quicken, Roden-Quicken-Royan, Roynetree, Sorb Apple, Thor's Helper, Whitty, Witchbane
Rue	Garden Rue, Herb of Repentance, Weasel, Rewe and Herb of Grace
Safflower	Dyer's Saffron, Bastard Saffron, Saffer
Sage	Sawge, Salvia, Clear Eye, Meadow Sage
Sassafras	Saloop, Ague Tree, Cinnamon Wood, Root Beer Tree

Common Name	Folk Name
Savory	Satyrs, Summer Savory, Winter Savory
Saw Palmetto	Palmetto, Cabbage Palm, Sabal Sabal Serrulata
Sheep's Sorrel	Fairy Bells, Field Sorrel, Oseille
Shepherd's Purse	Shepherd's Heart, Pickpurse, Casewort, Mother's Heart
Skullcap	Skul, Virginian Skull Cap, Mad-dog Skull Cap, Scullcap
Slippery Elm	Red Elm, Moose Elm, Indian Elm
Snapdragon	Head of Toad, Calf's Snout, Dog's Mouth, Lion's Lips, Toad's Mouth, Rabbit's Lips
Snowdrop	Fair Maid of February, Emblem of Early Spring, Mary's Tapers, Maids of February, Bulbous Violet, Candlemas Bells'
Solomon's Seal	Lady's Seals, Sealwort, Saint Mary's Seal, Drop Berry, Fo-ti, Sealroot
Southernwood	Our Lord's Wood, Old Man, Maiden's Ruin, Lad's Love, Boy's Love, Appleringie, Garderobe Herb, Garden Sagebrush, European Sage
Spearmint	Santa Maria, Spear, Horse Mint, Brown Mint, Green Mint, Our Lady's Mint, Mackerel Mint, Mismin

Common Name	Folk Name
Speedwell	Bird's Eye, Common Field-speedwell, Billy Bright-eye, Common Gypsyweed, Paul's Betony, Groundhele
Spiderwort	Trinity Flower, Bluejacket, Cow Slobber, Spider Lily, Indian Paint, Widow's Tears, Moses in the Bulrushes, Dayflower and Trinity Flower
Spikenard	Indian Roo, Spignet, Life of Man, Old Man's Root, Pettymorell, Indian Spikenard
St. John's Wort	Amber Touch-and-Heal, Goatweed, Rosin Rosie, Ear of a Goat, Klamath Weed
Sycamore	Ghosts of the forest, False Plane-tree, Great Maple, Scottish Maple, Mount Maple, Buttonwood, Mock-plane, Celtic Maple
Tansy	Buttons, Bitter Buttons, Cow Bitter and Golden Buttons
Tarragon	Little Dragon, Dragonwort, Green Dragon
Thyme	Running Thyme, Shepherd's Thyme, Mother of Thyme, Orange Thyme, Balsam Thyme
Toadflax	Toad, Rabbits, Ramsted, Yellow Toadflax, Butter and Eggs
Tuberose	Spanish Arbor Vine, Mistress of the Night, Minnieroot, Fever Root, Snapdragon Root and Sheep Potato
Turmeric	Curcuma, Indian Saffron

Common Name	Folk Name
Unicorn Root	Colic Root , Star Grass, Ague-root, True Unicorn's Root, Devil's Bit
Uva Ursi	Bearberry, Kinnikinnick , Pinemat Manzanita, Bear's Grape, Berry on the Vine
Valerian	All-Heal, Amantilla, Bloody Butcher, Capon's Trailer, Cat's Valerian, English Valerian, Cut finger, Vandal Root
Verbena	Herb of the Cross, Wild Hyssop, Vervain
Walnut	Caucasian Walnut, English Walnut, Tree of Evil, Carya, Walnoot Gender
Waterlily	Beaver Root, Cow Lily, Scatterdock, Toad Lily, Cow Cabbage
White Poppy	Opium Poppy, Mawseed
Wild Carrot	Birds Nest Weed, Devils Plague
Wild Cherry	Wild Cherry Bark , Black Cherry, Chokecherry, Virginia Prune Bark

Common Name	Folk Name
Wild Yam	Colic Root, Rheumatism Root
Willow	Tree of Enchantment, Witch's Tree, Salicyn Willow, Saille, Sally, Withe, Withy, Witches' Aspirin, Osier, Tarvos Tree, Sough Tree
Witch Hazel	Spotted Alder, Winterbloom, Snapping Hazelnut
Woodruff	Wild Baby's Breath, Winterbloom, Sweet Woodruff
Yarrow	Nosebleed Plant, Allheal, Angel Flower, Soldier's Woundwort and Squirrel's Taile

Folk Names of Appalachian Trees

Man's deeply sacred connection to trees is universal. Many religious traditions have a "Tree of Life" explaining creation in more than one physical plane and transition in more than one spiritual struggle. Age, death and renewal are revealed through the example of the deciduous (leaf shedding) trees cycling life through the seasons; where as evergreen trees traditionally represents life being everlasting or eternal.

Bitternut – Hickory

Sweet Elm or Elven – Elm

Tree of Evil, Walnoot and Acorn of Jupiter - Walnut

Lime tree, Linden - Basswood

Quaking Tree or Abbey Tree – Poplar

Lily Tree – Tulip Poplar

Omen Tree, Persian Apple - Peach

Feg or Billy goat fig - Fig

Bok or Boke - Beech

Tanbark or Weeping Spruce - Hemlock

Whipple-Tree or Dog Tree - Dogwood

Mazer or Maser Tree – Maple

God's Fruit or Pessemin - Persimmon

Balsam - Fir

Styrax or Sweetgum – Gum

Tanner's Bark or Jove's Nuts – Oak

Lady of the Woods – Birch

Plume tree – Plum

Conker, Horse Chestnut, Spanish Chestnut, Bark Bongay – Buckeye

Fairy Tree – Elder

Plane or Buttonwood – Sycamore

Tree of Chasity – Hawthorn

Gray Beard of the Swamp – Bald Cypress

Hoop Ash – Ash

Quick beam or Rowan-berry – Rowan

Silver Branch or Tree of Love – Apple

Tree of Death – Cypress

Bat's Wings, Christ's thorn, Holy Tree - Holly

Coll – Hazel

Sharon Fruit, Nature's Candy - Persimmon

Tree of Death or World Tree – Yew

Sweet Bay, Beaver Tree – Magnolia

Osier or Saugh Tree - Willow

King of the Waxing Year – Pine

Tale of Two Trees

The Appalachian settlers from Europe have much to thank the Cherokee, Shawnee and other native peoples for. Their experience in the use of herbal medicines and survival skills taught the settlers how to adapt to mountain life. Listed below are two trees common in the mountainous area of the Appalachians and can feed, clothe, provide warmth, produce good drinking water, wood materials to build with, waterproofing, insulation, and could be used to create utensils, toys, and medicines in folk healing.

The Water Birch Tree

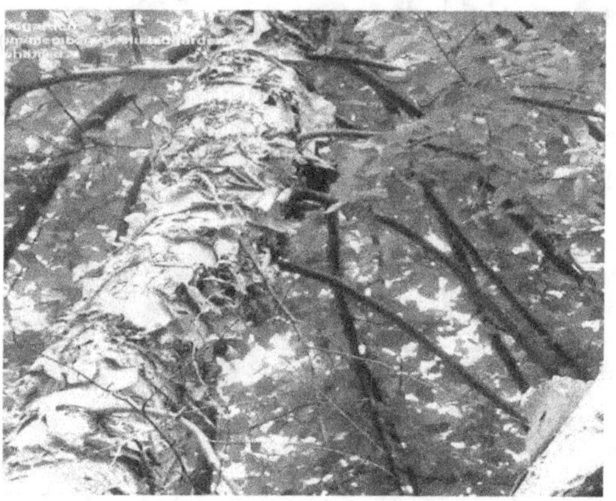

The water birch is one of the most useful trees in the mountains. With bright yellow leaves in the fall and a silvery bark and red twigs in the winter, these trees are usually found in clumps near rivers and streams and can live up to three hundred years. When young, their pinkish bark is easy to peel off into sheets. As it gets older, the bark darkens and becomes thicker.

The durable wood is excellent for furniture making. Sheets of the flexible bark can create a variety of things from cups, plates, boxes, eating utensils, bowls (receptacles are able to boil liquids on campfire coals without burning up), writing paper, lampshades and toys.

In addition, if you are lost and have no water, the tree can be tapped. River birch produces a sweet sap that can be a refreshing drink or it can also be boiled down into a syrup. If fermented, sap is also used to make birch beer or vinegar.

There is more to this list. The outer thin, papery bark is excellent for starting fires. The inner bark of the tree can be eaten as can the tops of its branches and young leaves. The root bark is used as a flour substitute.

You can harvest oil from the bark that can be used as a glue. Take a small, unlined aluminum can and bury it in the ground. Make sure the cup area is completely clean. Take a larger unlined can and put four to five holes around the center of it through the inside of the can. Pack it tightly with strips of birch bark filling it three quarters full. Make sure it has a tight lid so that it can seal the heat in. Place the larger can over the smaller one and pack soil around it until the larger can is one-fourth of the way covered in dirt. Build a fire around the larger can, packing coals around it and on top the lid. Leave it in the fire for three to four hours. Scrape coals and dirt away from the larger container. Gently lift it away from the smaller can. Pull smaller can out of the ground to finish cooling. The oil will have leaked into the smaller can through the holes in the larger. The oil secreted from the bark is tar-like and sticky. Great on leather for waterproofing and good as a glue.

Native Americans used the outer and waterproof inner bark for making temporary housing and in canoe making. Turned inside out, birch bark along with beeswax was once used to waterproof canoes. The rootlets of black spruce were used to sew and tie the pieces together. It is easy enough to do if you have a fire or a place to warm water.

Fire or warm water can make the bark bendable for bowls and baskets. Warm water can help you soften the thicker bark, so you can peel the layers for paper or to make strips for weaving baskets.

Here's how:

Take a piece of softened bark and fold it into squares. Unfold slightly and mark the inside corners of the bark with pencil. Pinch the ends of the bark to make the corners of the box. Once you get the shape you wish, bind it together by making small holes around the top of the box and threading string, rootlets or leather through it. You can also hold it together by placing sticks or twigs through the holes. You can cook (place on coals, not over fire) and eat out of these boxes without a problem.

 **Birch Box**

It has also been used for medical purposes; tea made from the twigs and leaves are loaded with vitamin C, calcium and manganese and eases aches and pains much like an aspirin. The oil is used as an anti-inflammatory and an analgesic. The leaves were originally used either chewed or as an infusion for the treatment of dysentery. The water from boiled bark is used as a wash for poison ivy.

Eastern White Pine

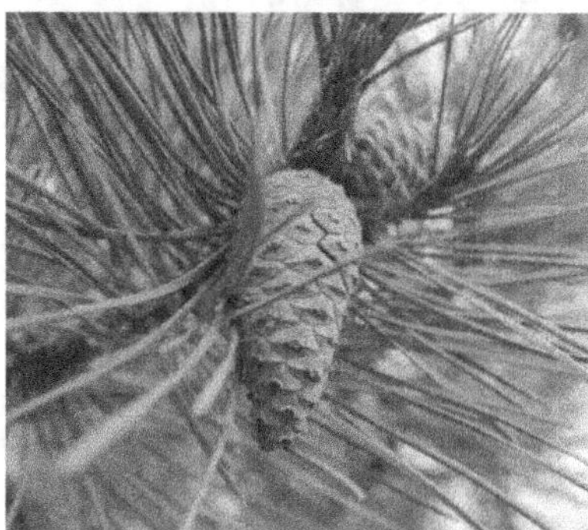

The eastern white pine is one of the most common trees growing throughout the Appalachian mountain range. Its dark gray bark and needle packets in bundles of five characterize the eastern white pine. If you look closely at the needles, you will see a fine white strip giving this pine its name.

The wood is used as one of the most common home construction materials in the northeastern part of the United States. The tree material is also used in carving and shipbuilding. The pine has a long lifespan and has been known to live for as long as five hundred years.

This remarkable tree has multiple uses. Used for waterproofing, the heated resin can also be mixed with charcoal, powdered eggshells, sand or plant material to make a strong epoxy. Its resin is flammable and is great for quick-starting fires. The melted resin is used for lamps and candles. It has even been used as a type of chewing gum. Besides food and tea, pine needles make a great insulation. Boiled needles produce a green dye. Surface layer roots, are used as cord for tying.

It was used by Native Americans as a "medicine tree" for hundreds of years. The turpentine extracted from the resin made a great antiseptic and diuretic. It dilates the blood vessels and brings blood to the surface of the skin. It protects wounds and helps them to heal. Drinking pine needle tea expels parasites from the body. A poultice made from the inner bark used on the chest can break up phlegm and heal wounds. Very high in vitamin C, tea from the pine needles treats colds, coughs and other respiratory ailments. The powdered wood was once used as a type of "baby powder" to keep infants from chaffing and was used on newborn babies to heal their navels.

As a food for survival, the pine nuts, needles, inner layer of the bark, and the male pollen anthers that are collected during the spring, are used and can be eaten fresh. Bark flour can be made by peeling off the bark's inner layer and allowing the pieces to dry. Once dried, it is ground into a flour. Mixed with other flours, it can extend their use.

Planting by the Signs

"If the moon shows like a silver shield,

You may not be afraid to reap your field;

But if she rises haloed round,

Soon we'll tread on deluged ground."

-Scotch farm saying

Farmers and breeders are used to consulting *The Old Farmer's Almanac* for lunar times, planetary alignments, frost dates, planting seasons, or the beginning of animal breed production. Many look to it as a reference book for the best times for wildcrafting, healing or spell work. **It is best to acquire an Almanac for a better understanding of this system.**

Planting Days by Sign

****When trying to understand how this system works, you need to evaluate the environment around you. Climate, food and culture will make a big difference.**

Each sign or quarter moon lists the best times for other specific things to be done as well. Check accordingly. An Almanac is a good thing to have if you are interested in learning more about this.

Water Signs

For astrological signs of Pisces, Scorpio and Cancer:

During the first or second quarter of the moon, plant leafy annuals. Be sure to saturate the soil when watering lawns, bushes or trees. Plants absorb more water during a full moon so, this can make it doubly so. Spinach, Lettuces, Creasy greens and Chard are some leafy, watery-signed annuals planted when the moon is a water sign.

Earth Signs

For astrological signs of Virgo, Capricorn and Taurus:

The element of earth is associated with roots and the things that grow beneath the ground. Beets, carrots and horseradish are basic root crops planted during the third quarter phase of the moon. For good growth, transplant bushes and trees during this phase.

Air Signs

For astrological signs of Aquarius, Gemini and Libra:

When the moon is in the sign of air, it is time to cultivate and harvest. Air signs that pass through the time of waning moon promote fertileness and growth in vines, tubers, herbs and roots.

Fire Signs

For astrological signs of Sagittarius, Aries and Leo:

The signs are barren and dry. Farmers prune back their plants for next season. This is a good time for growing fruit and seed plants. If you want to store or preserve fruits and vegetables, do it in the fourth quarter.

Astrological Planting Days

During each lunar month, we go through days that associate with all twelve signs of the zodiac and can relate to the different parts of plants. Some days are great for **seed** planting; others **leaf**, as well as **flower** and **root**.

Aries, Leo and Sagittarius - Elements of fire, relating to growth and creativity, great days to plant **seed**.

Taurus, Virgo and Capricorn - Elements of the earth, relating to structure and physical form, great days to plant **roots**.

Gemini, Libra and Aquarius - Elements of air, relating to colorful, creative imagination and ideas, great days to plant **flowers**.

Cancer, Scorpio and Pisces - Elements of water, relating to growth and fullness, great days to plant things that live above ground. These days are **leaf** days and are good days for top of the soil, leaf-growing plants.

Good advice for Planting and Harvesting

* **P**lant in proper moon sign and harvest under same sign. Try to avoid hours during eclipses, nodes or perigee.

* **D**o not plant or cultivate the soil twelve hours before or after an eclipse.

* **W**hen the moon descends (3pm-3am) or during a waxing moon, transplants plants. This will help build a good root system.

* **A** good time to take softwood cuttings for grafting is between 3am and 3pm when the moon is ascending, and the sap is high. Cuttings of hardwood are better grafted during the moon's descend (3pm-3am).

* **P**rune under a waning moon between the hours of 3pm-3am. Water levels will be low in the plants.

* **I**t is not good to prune on leaf days.

* **P**rune trees during a descending moon. It will help heal any cut or broken bark on the tree.

* **D**uring an ascending, waxing moon (3am-3pm), graft softwood. Hardwoods are grafted during descending moon times (3pm-3am).

* **F**ruit picked during a new moon will store well.

* **F**ruit picked during a full moon should be eaten quickly. There is a lot of moisture in the soil during this lunar time and the water content in the crops will be high. This causes fruits and vegetables to ripen faster and rot.

* **H**arvest your crops during ascending moon times.

* **H**arvest crops early in the morning to get the best of their qualities.

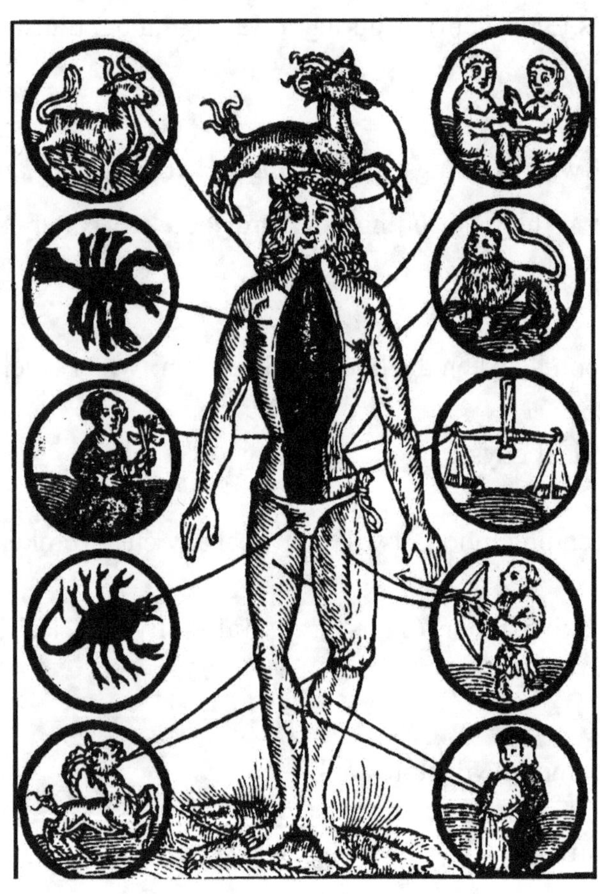

In 17th century Italy, Italian physicians developed a medical system called Iatromathematics (medicine mathematics). The prime influences of this system came from the scientific writings of Aristotle on animal motion and Leonardo da Vinci in his studies of the human body. Iatromathematics also incorporated the influences of the sun, moon, planets as well as astrological signs and the natural elements for use in diagnosing illnesses. Many physicians recognized the body "humors" through astrological or planetary influences. – CSB

Choosing Herbs According to the Signs

Aries- March 21 - April 19- Aries rules the head, eyes and face, and is a **Fire** sign ruled by the planet Mars. Plants in this sign usually have thorns or a rough texture, a bitter or spicy taste and reddish color. Being high in iron, they purify the blood or stimulate the adrenal glands. Some herbs ruled by Aries:

Nettles, coriander, burdock root, calendula, gentian, mustard, geranium, milk thistle, anise, hyssop, horseradish, poppies, cayenne pepper, red pepper, red roses, St. John's wort, red clover, tulips, wormwood, marjoram, amaryllis, hollyhock, cowslip, onion, garlic, leeks, tiger lily, impatiens, sarsaparilla, hops, tarragon, ginger

Taurus- April 20 - May 20- Taurus rules the throat, thyroid, tonsils, neck, upper back and ears and is an **Earth** sign ruled by the planet Venus. Plants under this sign have showy flowers or strong fragrances. Having a high copper content, these herbs are used as preventatives for sore throats and hoarseness, upper back issues, and neck problems. Some herbs ruled by Taurus:

Spinach, hyssop, licorice, vervain, feverfew, peas, violet, white potato, sweet potato, sweet william, gourds, angelica, artichoke, lily of the valley, olive, aster, sweet pea, grape, apple, marshmallow, sage, fig, lilac, apricot, rose, fenugreek, anise, lily of the valley, sweet pea, slippery elm, pomegranate, daisies, strawberries, foxglove, lavender, mallow, dandelion

Gemini- May 21 - June 20- Gemini is ruled by the planet Mercury and is an **Air** sign. This planet rules the lungs, shoulders, arms and hands. The herbs associated with this sign help build up the lungs and respiratory system, are usually fuzzy or hairy in nature, and can have divided stems or leaves. Some herbs ruled by Gemini:

Lemongrass, daffodil, mullein, hyssop, azalea, parsnips, lemon balm, carrots, honeysuckle, lobelia, elecampane, vervain, woodbine, bergamot, yarrow, meadowsweet, dill, milk thistle, fennel, lilac, skullcap, lavender, fenugreek, licorice, valerian, oats, chrysanthemum, endive, lily-of-the-valley

Cancer- June 21 – July 22- Cancer rules the breasts, stomach, liver and diaphragm. A **Water** sign ruled by the Moon, Cancer herbs help aid digestion and are known to affect the subconscious mind. Many of these plants are found around water and usually have a rounded or a swollen look due to a large moisture content. Some herbs ruled by Cancer:

Mushrooms, jasmine, watermelon, lily, pumpkin, peppermint, spearmint, white roses, morning glory, lemon balm, Brussels sprouts, carnation, iris, broccoli, cabbage, cauliflower, pear, endive, kale, magnolia, parsley, lettuce, watercress, turnip, chickweed, sweet potato, cantaloupe, cucumber, gourds, squash, banana, broccoli, apple, daisy, water lilies, hyssop, morning glory, geranium, lotus, opium poppy, cauliflower, agrimony, verbena

Leo- July 23 - Aug. 22- A **Fire** sign ruled by the Sun, Leo governs the heart in the human body. Plants aligned with this sign are usually large and have a golden or orange color. Leaves can be heart-shaped or radiating. They energize the body and help regulate blood pressure. Some herbs ruled by Leo:

Chamomile, peony, mint, saffron, calendula, cinnamon, orange, anise, sunflower, Chinese cabbage, hawthorn, corn, borage, collards, mugwort, peppers, mustard, parsley, Swiss chard, St. John's wort, poppy, eyebright, okra, marigolds, peppers, dahlia, pineapple, dill, fennel, orange, passion flower, bay, ginger, grapefruit, angelica, olive, coconut, Chinese cabbage, calendula

Virgo- Aug. 23 - Sept. 22- An **Earth** sign ruled by Mercury, these plants are high in potassium and are used for digestion and to calm the nerves. Flowers are brightly colored and have small leaves and stems. Some herbs ruled by Virgo:

Ivy, valerian, endive, aster, carrots, plantain, blackberry, parsnips, barley, dill, woodbine oats, Narcissus, violet, sage, fennel, St. John's wort, patchouli, wheat, lavender, marjoram, licorice, parsley, millet, fenugreek, dill, skullcap, chrysanthemum, fern, rye, oak moss, lemon balm

Libra- Sept. 23 – Oct. 22- An **Air** sign ruled by Venus, it aligns with the kidneys, the adrenal system and helps keep the physical body balanced. Some herbs ruled by Libra:

Broccoli, corn silk, eggplant, yarrow, spinach, angelica, peas, pansy, sweet potato, violet, artichoke, apricot, apple, mint, thyme, fig, parsley, plum, gardenia, grape, daisy, strawberry, juniper, primrose, pansy, hydrangea, thyme, cleavers

Scorpio- Oct. 23 – Nov. 21- The energy of Mars and Pluto rule this **Water** sign. Used for the maintenance of the reproductive organs, hormones and women's cycles, these plants are found in well-hidden, remote or dark places. Many of these herbs have thorns and can be a reddish color. Some herbs ruled by Scorpio:

Mushroom, cramp bark, heather, saw palmetto, ginger, peppers, holly, pennyroyal, rhubarb, ginseng, raspberry leaf, leek, onions, chives, pepper, garlic, horseradish, hibiscus, radish, mustard, honey-suckle, basil, wormwood, gardenia

Sagittarius- Nov. 22 – Dec. 21- A **Fire** sign ruled by Jupiter that governs the liver in the human body. These herbs have a high percentage of silica in them. Some herbs ruled by Sagittarius:

Red roses, wild yam, carnations, asparagus, mint, peony, nutmeg, jasmine, hyssop, rhubarb, horsetail, crocus, beet, tomato, feverfew, turnip, clematis, watercress, olive, sage, calendula, Oregon grape root

Capricorn- Dec. 22 – Jan. 19- Aligning with Saturn, the **Earth-**signed herbs in Capricorn are slow growing, woody, and usually do not smell or taste very good to people. They are high in calcium. Some herbs ruled by Capricorn:

African violet, spinach, horsetail, mushroom, baby's breath, beet, parsnips, henbane, barley, thyme, black poppy, horsetail, rue, rye, nightshade, snowdrop, mullein, sarsaparilla, shepherd's purse, love-lies-bleeding, comfrey

Aquarius- Jan. 20 – Feb. 18- An **Air** sign ruled by Uranus, these herbs support the circulatory system and help heal the nervous system. Some herbs ruled by Aquarius:

Valerian, catnip, cinnamon, spinach, cloves, beet, rye, passion flower, barley, spikenard, parsnip, frankincense, aloe, myrrh, hops, trillium, skullcap, chamomile, orchid, kava kava, gladiolus

Pisces- Feb. 19 – Mar. 20- Ruled by Neptune and Jupiter, these **Water** sign herbs are either bulbous or grow near or in water, and help build up the immune system, have an antibacterial effect or can expand different states of awareness. Some herbs ruled by Pisces:

Golden seal, narcissus, eyebright, asparagus, yarrow, endive, chaparral, mushroom, rhubarb, orchid, tomato, seaweed, mugwort, watercress, echinacea, olive, calendula, anise hyssop, jasmine, lilac, water lily, nutmeg, poppy, kava kava, clematis, oatstraw, wisteria, skullcap, lilac, anise.

Poultices, Tinctures, Tonics, Ointment, Oils and Tea

Learning to live on the land requires a lot of trial and effort. The use of natural materials, such as plants and resins were vital for medicines, beauty aids and cleansers. Many people also rely on clays, oils and animal materials for dyes and spell work.

*****This comes with a warning: Make positive identification of materials used, and always check with a physician before consuming wild plants. Some people may be allergic. Make sure you can tolerate them before using.**

Poultice

Crushed into a pulp or made into a paste, an herbal poultice is spread directly onto the surface of the skin and held in place with gauze or a clean cloth. It is then wrapped around the area to keep the natural medicine from rubbing off. To prevent leakage, plastic wrap can be used. When the wrap is changed, fresh material is used, and old material is thrown away.

The healing actions of a poultice change with temperature. A warm or hot poultice can increase circulation to the area, while a cold poultice can help soothe redness and inflammation. Ginger, Ginkgo or Cayenne Pepper can be added to increase blood circulation to an area.

Most poultice recipes are quite simple. Select a leaf from the plant you wish to use. Roll or knead the material between your fingers so that it is crushed and has a moist feeling. Smooth the crushed leaf over the affected area and wrap it with a bandage. Change every few hours with a fresh leaf if desired. Remove the bandage after a few hours or so, to let the area breathe for a bit.

Besides herbs, other materials from nature are also used. Honey from bees promotes healing when used on wounds and burns. Brown grass spider webs are collected in the morning when the dew is on the grass and are useful for closing wounds. Clay can draw poisons and stings out of the skin. Human urine is used to kill off foot fungus. Mountain people were known to make extensive use of the natural world.

When making a poultice, fresh herbs are best but if all you have at hand is dried herbs, take the dried material and add just enough hot water to get them moist. Grind dried roots into a powder. When chopped, chewed, ground or laid bare, the natural world can produce all the medicines we need.

Some Simple Poultices

Banana – A piece of the peel placed on a splinter and wrapped in a bandage will draw the splinter out.

Black Mustard (seeds) – It is quickly absorbed in the skin, causing the blood vessels to dilate. Used for healing below-surface inflammation.

Bentonite Clay – Place on spider bites to draw the poison out. Good for eczema, too.

Cankeroot (root and rhizomes) – These are chewed, raw or boiled. Used for canker sores, fever blisters, irritation and a sore throat.

Cattail (bottom 4-6 inches of the stem) – In the stem's layers, there is a jelly-like substance. This substance is used on the skin as an antiseptic.

Catnip (leaf) – This herb is chewed and placed on the skin to relieve bug bites. Great for toothache, too.

Chickweed (leaves and stems) – The herb is made into a paste and applied to the skin to draw out splinters.

Comfrey (leaf and root) – Good for bruises, bedsores, burns and infections. Speeds healing. Do not use if you have liver problems.

Dandelion (leaf) – Used to draw out splinters.

Epsom Salt or Salt – Use as a poultice for abscesses.

Fig – Mash up the fruit of a ripe fig and place it on a bo il to draw or heal it up.

Honey – It is applied to the skin, for burns and getting rid of scar tissue.

Horsetails (Bottlebrush) (stems) – This herbal poultice is applied to wounds to stop bleeding.

Nettle (leaf) – Inhale the powdered leaves of the plant to stop a nosebleed.

Plantain (plant or root) – Chopped or chewed, this poultice placed on the skin is used to draw out venom from bug bites, snakebites or insect stings. Good for blisters, boils and splinters, too.

Tobacco (leaf) – If chewed and placed on a bee sting, it draws out the sting and the poison.

Virginia Snake (root) – Used for snakebite – The chewed root is applied to the wound.

Wintergreen (leaf) – This is applied directly to the skin and is used for rheumatism and lower back pain.

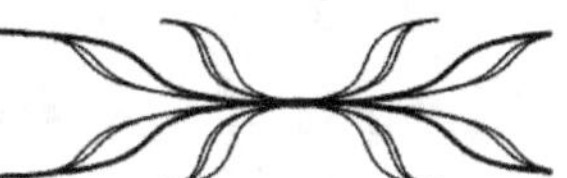

Common Methods Used for the Extraction of Herbal Medicines
Ways to Create Tincture, Tonic, Oil and Tea

** **Note:** The morning is the best time to harvest herbs while the leaves still have lots of flavor. **

Tincture - You will need a clean jar with a tight seal, a piece of cheesecloth to strain the herbs through, spring water, and a clear alcohol (such as Vodka or Everclear) with at least forty-five percent alcohol content.

Use fresh herbs if you can. Fill the jar with ½ herbs to ½ alcohol. Seal the lid tightly and let sit for 28 days. Strain off and use.

Decoction – Produced from hardier parts of the plants such as roots, stems, bark and rhizomes that need to be boiled in water. The water contains the extraction of the plant.

Maceration – The process of softening materials by soaking in a liquid. Oil is usually the base. Place in an airtight container in a warm sunny area for up to three weeks. Strain out old herb material and replace with fresh until the oil or liquid is consistent.

Infusion – You need to steep plants in hot water or warm oil to draw out their beneficial properties. Tea is an example of infusion.

Thanks to Psaguer

Some Simple Tonics and Washes

Bluets plant - A great rinse for killing head lice; clears sunspots, freckles and other blemishes.

Fennel - A good tonic to keep the skin tightened. Anti-wrinkle wash.

Gentian - Is applied to the skin for treating cancer and unhealed wounds.

Goldenseal - Used as an antiseptic mouthwash, laxative tonic and vaginal douche.

Hawthorn berry - Used as a heart tonic.

Inkberry - The berries are brewed to make a brandy.

Kudzu - The tonic is used as a wash for healing psoriasis.

Motherwort - The wash is used for treating psoriasis, eczema and shingle irritation.

Plantain - A good wash used for eczema, rashes and sunburn.

Thuja - Used on the skin as a wash for joint and muscle pain.

Wintergreen leaf - A wash used for sore muscles, and lower back pain and in the relief of rheumatism.

Herbal Ingredients used in making Blood Tonic: Blackstrap molasses, figs, cherries, black currants or raisins, beets, cooked onion, mulberries, bilberry, raspberry, blackberries and black grapes.

Ointment or Salve

***Fresh herbs need to sit for around twelve hours after cutting before making ointments (salves) as well as oils.** This keeps the extra moisture out that can cause the materials to go bad. Dried herbs and roots work better ground.

To make Ointment:

1oz. of herbs (fresh or dry ground) per **3 cups of oil** (olive, unscented almond or sunflower oil)

Use beeswax or soft paraffin to keep the ointment consistent.

To use Gum benzoin- 1 drop of benzoin per ounce of product; it is a good preservative for topical medicinal products or skin lotions; do not use in food.

Some Simple Ointments or Salves

Arnica – Topical; ointment is used for the relief of pain on sprains and bruises but should not be used on broken skin.

Bee Balm - A well-known ointment used for treating acne, eczema and psoriasis.

Black Poplar - Balm of Gilead – Made into a salve, it is applied to the body to heal burns, boils and hemorrhoids.

Calendula – Ointment made from the plant's flowers is antiseptic and antifungal. Great for cuts and treating infected wounds.

Chamomile - An all-purpose salve that treats bites, stings, wounds, itching and eczema.

Comfrey - This ointment encourages rapid healing of the skin and cell growth.

Elder Leaf - Used as an anti-inflammatory, this salve can ease the pain of sprains and bruises.

Rhubarb Root - This ointment is applied to the skin to treat cold sores.

St. John's Wort - This herbal ointment is used for nerve pain and scar reduction caused by burns. An anti-viral, it also is used for shingles lesions.

Virginia Snake Root - Ointment can be used on infected toes and finger nails, eczema and slow healing cuts.

Infused Oil

***Fresh herbs need to sit for around twelve hours after cutting before making oils.** This keeps the extra moisture out that can cause the materials to go bad. Dried herbs and roots work better ground.

Mix 1-ounce herb to 3 ounces of olive, unscented almond or sunflower oil. Blend well and seal in a dark glass bottle. If the herbs are fresh, store in a cool dark area. If the herbs are dry, a dark, warm area is better. Replace the herbs every 10 to 12 days until it has the proper scent. Strain and bottle when finished. Keep finished bottles of oil out of direct sunlight.

Black Walnut oil - This oil is used to expel parasitic worms from the body when ingested. Also used in the treatment of viral warts, acne, eczema, psoriasis and poison ivy.

Castor oil - Used to tighten stretch marks on the skin. Removes moles and skin tags, too.

Clove oil - For oral and skin infections; it is antibacterial, antifungal, antiseptic and analgesic.

Dill oil - It is a known bug repellent; successful in the treatment of head lice and for shrinking hemorrhoids.

Lavender oil - Used to draw out stings and poison from spider bites. It's great for burns, cuts and other wounds.

Mullein oil - Antiviral oil used to soothe earaches.

Oregano oil - Improves the blood and kills intestinal parasites if ingested. The oil is antibacterial and antifungal. Relieves athlete's foot, ringworm, canker sores, dandruff, warts, rosacea, psoriasis and varicose veins.

Tarragon oil - Kills bacteria on the skin, reduces body odor and fights bad breath.

Thuja oil - Used for the treatment of cancer and other skin diseases; removes warts, relieves joint pain and can be used as an insect repellent.

Wintergreen oil - Kills germs on the skin, and relieves muscle pain and reduces swelling.

Chicory or Dandelion Root Coffee

Once cleaned, place the roots on baking sheets and put them in the oven at 250 degrees for about 3-4 hours. Move them around every now and then to dry them evenly. To darken, turn up heat to 325 degrees for 35 minutes. When the roots finish roasting, they should be crisp. Let cool and grind up. Use about two teaspoons per cup. Bring to a boil and then simmer for 4 minutes.

Flowers and leaves of both plants are eaten as well. Both wild herbs have immune boosting qualities and helps relieve stress. Make sure you are harvesting away from any areas with car exhaust or areas that have been sprayed with pesticides.

*** Harvest roots in the fall. Wash and clean thoroughly. Let dry and chop into small pieces.**

Tea

To make a good herbal tea, boil your water but **do not boil your herbs.** It is best to let the water sit for a minute or two before adding your herbal mixture. This way, none of the healing properties from the herbs are boiled out, and you have a good consistency. Use 1 big teaspoon dried or ground herbs to 10 ounces of water. If using fresh herbs, use 1 large pinch. Let the tea sit for 3-5 minutes; then strain.

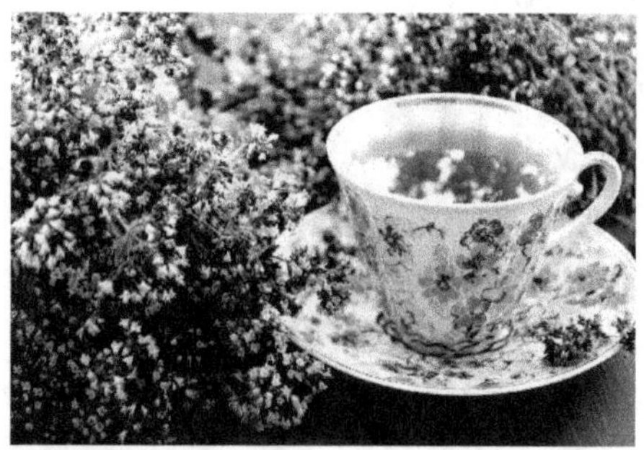

Thanks to Mareefe

Examples of Healing Teas and Gargles

Apple tea - Known for building the immune system, Apple tea is also used for curing headache, reducing stress, and reducing constipation. It is an anti-inflammatory and can level cholesterol.

Alfalfa tea - A known diuretic, it is used for arthritis pain, problems, and high cholesterol. Drinking the tea can also reduce bad breath and body odor.

Basil tea - Besides drinking the tea, basil can be used as a wash in infected areas to kill germs. Good to use for insect stings and 1bites. Used for cough and colds and is known to lower stress and blood sugar. Combats PMS and bloating.

Bee Balm tea - This tea is used for treating colds, fevers, headaches, nasal congestion, and sore throat. Good for the stomach and is said to ease menstrual pain.

Catnip tea - Cures insomnia by acting as a sedative. Relieves stress, soothing nervous disorders. Known to treat indigestion, intestinal cramps, and diarrhea. Good for colic. It can induce menstruation.

Chive tea - Used for its antibacterial properties in order to detoxify the body. Promotes good health during a pregnancy. Beneficial for the digestive track and is believed to prevent some types of cancer.

Dandelion tea - Builds the blood and is used to boost the immune system. Cleans the liver, urinary track and prevents gallstones. A laxative. Good for skin and aching muscles.

Dill tea - This tea is used to fight diabetes, to boost the immune system and is a possible treatment in epilepsy. Known to lower cholesterol. Prevents intestinal gas, and stomach acid secretions. Gets rid of hiccups, stomach gas, indigestion and bad breath when chewed.

Fennel tea - Fennel tea eases and soothes colicky babies and is known to increase milk flow in mothers. Eases menstrual cramps and helps with symptoms of menopause and PMS. Lowers blood pressure and treats anemia. Eliminates hiccups and soothes indigestion. Alleviates bad breath when chewed.

Feverfew tea - Infertility and problems with menstruation in women. Used for fevers, migraine headaches, nausea and vomiting. Eases the pain of rheumatoid arthritis. Used as a wash for psoriasis.

Ginger Root tea - Relieves the stress of morning and motion sickness. Builds the immune system and lowers blood sugar. Helps suppressed menstruation. Promotes sweat to clear illness from the body.

Goldenseal tea - Promotes healing in upper respiratory tract infections. Eases hay fever. Used for digestive disorders, colitis, diarrhea, constipation and hemorrhoids. Cleans the liver.

Holy Thistle tea - Good for detoxifying and purifying. An herbal drink for cleansing the circulation system of bacteria and deleting fat build-up in the blood.

Hawthorn berry tea - Traditionally used for treating heart diseases. The herb can be used as a diuretic, antiseptic, sedative, astringent, and an antioxidant. It boosts immunity.

Inkberry tea - Called **Appalachian tea** – Roasted and dried leaves were originally brewed by Native American Indians. The leaves are loaded with vitamin A and C and are used as a laxative or as an antioxidant for purging.

Innocence's tea (Folk name) - Bluets plant – A blood cleanser, it also strengthens the bladder, alleviates kidney problems, helps to prevent bed-wetting and eases cramps. The tea has been used as a gout treatment and is known to relieve constipation. Healers used it as a treatment for jaundice and other liver diseases.

Jasmine tea - Antibiotic and anti-inflammatory, the tea is used to boost the immune system. It's said to be able to reduce the risk of heart attack, and prevent diabetes as well as cancer. Boosts metabolism and improves digestion as well as soothing arthritic pain.

Juniper Berry tea - Known as a diuretic and is anti-inflammatory. Prevents bladder infection by killing bacteria. Used for digestive, kidney and fluid retention problems.

Kudzu tea - Good for upper respiratory tract infections, colds and hay fever. Eases diarrhea. Used for treating alcohol abuse.

Knapweed tea - Used in the treatment of broken veins, swelling, sore throat and sinus infection. Promotes healing of kidney problems and scabies infections.

Licorice root tea - Used for detoxifying the body and digestive system. Promotes healing of peptic ulcers. Eases asthma, bronchitis and nagging coughs.

Lemon Balm tea - Lemon Balm is used to treat nervous disorders, hyperthyroidism and indigestion. Good for depression and anxiety. Eases palpitations and tension headaches.

Motherwort tea - Used for expelling afterbirth. PMS treatment; used for cramps and promotes regular menstrual cycles. Healing agent for the uterus after childbirth.

Mullein tea - For treatment of colds and croup. Antiviral; has been used for the treatment of herpes, influenza, asthma and coughs.

Nettle tea - High in iron and Vitamin C, the tea is used to ease arthritis, rheumatism and is good for urinary tract infections. Nursing mothers drink this tea to promote milk flow.

Nasturtium tea - The tea is a natural antibiotic. Used for fighting bacteria, viruses and tumor growth. Helps to heal urinary tract infections. Prevents scurvy.

Onion tea - Kills infection and is an anti-fungal. Used to clear up sore throats. Used for clearing the arteries and helps reduce blood pressure. Used to rid sore throats. Relieves leg cramps. Reduces dandruff.

****Organic onions if possible; if not, wash with baking soda, rinse and let dry before use.**

Orris root tea - Anti-inflammatory; soothes the stomach. Used for bronchitis and chronic diarrhea. A great tea for sore throats and colds.

Plantain tea - Good for sore throats, mouth ulcers and respiratory infections. Promotes healthy liver and kidney function. Good for treating scalp problems.

Quack Grass tea - (Couch grass, witch grass, etc.) Rootstock is used for the tea. Used for inflammation, high blood pressure and fever. Clears bladder and kidney problems. Relieves water retention.

Raspberry tea - Used by some midwives to shorten and ease labors. Strengthens the uterus and pelvic muscles. Balances hormones and strengthens the walls of the uterus.

Rhubarb tea - Reduces pain from hemorrhoids. Used in treating constipation, diarrhea, and stomach pain and gastrointestinal bleeding.

Sassafras tea - Used in the treatment of urinary tract infections and swelling in the upper respiratory area. Helps relieve gout and arthritis.

Saw Palmetto tea - Used to treat impotence, infertility, inflammation and urinary tract infections. An antiseptic. Good for indigestion and promotes healing of respiratory infections.

Tarragon tea - Drink the tea before bed to help relieve anxiety and insomnia.

Thuja tea - Boosts the immune system and is good for respiratory tract infections as well as bacterial skin infections. Loosens phlegm.

Uva Ursi tea - Reduces bacteria in the urine. Urinary and Bladder and kidney infections. Reduces swelling. Eases bronchitis.   *****Use only in small amounts; do not use if pregnant.**

Virginia Snakeroot tea - Birthwort (Folk name) - A weak tea made from the stems of the plant was used to induce labor. Controls bacterial infections for faster healing. Reduces inflammation.

Willow bark tea - Used for thinning the blood and bring down swelling. Anti- viral and bacterial. Eases menstrual cramps, lower back and arthritis pain. Good for relieving fever, colds and flu.

Wintergreen tea - Wintergreen leaf is used to bring down fevers and ease colds. Good for ovarian pain and menstrual cramps. Pain and swelling. Also helps with lung conditions and kidney problems.

Yellow Dock tea - Used for detoxing, hormone and immune balance. Balances blood sugar and is great for general skin health.

Yellow Gentian tea - A true germ killer, it can be applied to the skin for wounds and skin cancers. It helps remove parasitic worms and is known to be able to restart menstrual cycles. The tea is used for fever, diabetes, and high blood pressure problems. Good for heartburn, too.

Natural Dyes, Soap and Candle Making

Practicality is important when you live in the mountains. Sometimes, you just have to create things yourself, in order to survive. If you can build something new or repurpose whatever is available, then you have something you can use.

Natural Dyes

M uted or vibrant colors are derived from roots, berries, leaves, bark, wood, fungi and lichens that are added to boiling water. This leaches out the chemicals needed to produce the shades and colors that dye yarn or cloth.

In traditional dyeing, natural mordants bind the dye to the cloth or yarn to fix or enhance the color. Some of the mordants that are used include: Tannin from oak bark, vinegar, stale urine, oak galls, potash and wood-ash liquor made by leaching wood ashes, natural alum, ammonia and salt and even fermenting fruit. A variety of colors and shades are produced from the same dye materials when using a different mordant. A mordant can be used either to pre-treat the cloth or yarn or to be added into the dye. Because of strong odors produced by the mixing of these chemicals, many people dyed their materials away from close living areas.

National Archives and Records Administration

Natural Dye Colors for Yarn and Cloth

Blue – Dogwood Bark, indigo, woad, elderberries, blueberries, purple grapes

Green – Nettles, sage, artichokes, sorrel roots, dock, spinach, tansy, fennel, peppermint leaves, betony, sunflower, grass, coltsfoot, horsetail, plantain, rosemary and peach leaves

Yellow – Yellow onion skin, mullein flowers, grape leaves, lilac flowers, yellow marigold flowers, wild apple bark, turmeric, yellow dock root, Queen Anne's lace root and dandelion flowers

Orange – Orange marigold flowers, chicory, yarrow, carrots and dandelion root

Red – Beet juice, pokeberries, red onion peel, sweet woodruff, St. John's wort, lady's bedstraw and safflower

Dark Red – Birch leaves and moss

Pink – Woad, cherries, bloodroot, red and pink rose petals, berries and sorrel

Red-purple – Basil leaves, red sumac berries, huckleberries, grapes and pokeweed berries

Red-Brown – Bamboo, hibiscus (red flowers) and bloodroot

Brown – Acorns, oak bark, walnut hulls, tea and coffee

Black – Oak galls, walnut hulls and gallberry

Gray-Black – Blackberries, iris root, poplar, elder and walnut hulls.

Soap Making

A list of what you need:

- **O**il or fat

- **S**oft Water or rainwater *Soft water can be made by putting sodium carbonate (soda ash) in it.

- **L**ye (Either by making homemade lye or buying some Red Devil lye) *** **When mixing, add lye to your water, not the other way around or you may have an explosion.**

Also Needed:

-- **L**arge stainless steel pots --

-- **U**tensils to stir with and/or a hand blender --

-- **L**arge towel or cloth --

-- **W**ax paper --

-- **P**aper Bags --

-- **S**oap Molds --

-- **V**inegar --

-- **R**ubber Safety Gloves --

-- **G**oggles; some people wear a mask, too --

Special Things you can add to your soaps:

-- **E**ssential oils --

-- **S**ynthetic scented oils --

-- **H**erbs, bark, fruit or spice (including dried flowers) --

Homemade Lye

Lye occurs naturally in nature by leaching rainwater through hardwood ashes. Some of the best hardwoods for lye making are ash, hickory, sugar maple, buckeye or beech. **If you are making your own lye at home, you will need a well-ventilated area as lye gives off fumes when mixed with water ****

To make your own lye at home, begin by boiling the ashes in a large pot for about a half hour. **Do not use an aluminum pot, as lye eats through aluminum.** Lye separates and forms on top of the water as the ashes boil. Before you skim the lye off the top, make certain to remove the pot from the burner and that the ash has settled to the bottom of the pot. Make sure you are using hardwood ashes as the softwood's resins do not mix with the fat. Do not allow the lye to encounter your skin. If this happens, use a wash of vinegar, then soap and water. Keep a bottle of vinegar nearby to neutralize the burning if it does. Let the lye set and cool.

In the soap-making process, lye is added to boiling water. Gently stir until mixed. It will create a lot of heat and fumes. That is normal. Once mixed, the lye and water mixture need a rest period to cool. Once cooled, around 130 degrees, it is then poured into the hot grease. The fat and oils neutralize the lye, making the soap safe to use. By gradually mixing the lye to a fat base, it creates a soft soap.

Caution: Repeated again:

"… Add water to lye and you may die!"

*****Add lye to your water, not water to the lye or you may have a violent reaction. *****

***** Wear gloves and protective goggles when mixing. *****

****

Rendering Fat and Mixing

You can use any type of fatty scraps or left-over oils. Place the scraps in a large pot until it is about half way full and heat it gently to render out the clean grease. While it is hot, add in the cooled lye and stir until it thickens. Boil down the liquid and stir the material until it has the right consistency. You can put a whole egg (with shell) on the top of the liquid when you think it is ready. If it is done, the egg will float.

Add the cooled lye mixture to the clean grease and stir with a whisk or a hand blender. Keep mixing slowly until the oil and lye liquid are well mixed. If you don't have a hand blender, it might take forty-five minutes or more to get it thick with a whisk; be patient. Once it achieves the required thickness, place a cover on the stainless steel pot and set it back on low heat for an hour.

Setting the Soap

Get a box that is two inches deep. It can be a small box for a bar or a large one that is sectioned. Place waxed paper on the bottom and sides of these "molds" so the soap will not stick. Pour the soap using a rubber spatula to spread it evenly. When it is set, it will still be soft. You can **"salt the soap"** to harden the bars you have poured. To do this you will want to use two and a half pints of salt to a five-gallon ratio of soap. Mix well. Place a top over the box when you are finished and wrap a large towel or cloth over to keep the heat inside. Leave it wrapped for twenty-four to thirty-six hours so it can start to cure and be cool enough to cut.

Once cooled, check your soap to make sure there are no problems. You have to make sure all of the lye has reacted, so the soap will not cause a reaction and burn you. Place to the side any soap that is separated on top with an oily layer or if the soda has heavy white patches on it as. It the soap has only a thin bit of white dusting, it is fine. Cut the soap into bars using equal pressure as you cut. You might want to use a small kitchen cleaver. One you have cut them, you will need to set them up for a least a month to cure them completely. Lay them somewhere the air can get to them. Place them on paper bags and turn them every two to three weeks until dry.

Healing herbal additives that give soaps a natural color:

Black Walnut Hull - Purple and black specks; dried and ground, for exfoliating

Alfalfa - Medium green color; dried and ground; good for skin, reduces stretch marks

Chlorophyll - Green color, powdered; deodorizing properties

Beet root powder - Bright yellow color; contains antioxidants

Cornmeal - Yellow color; exfoliating

Calendula - Yellow color; powdered or dried whole flowers; antifungal, anti-inflammatory, and antibacterial

Carrots -Yellow- Orange color; raw ground; contains beta carotene

Chamomile - Beige to yellow color; dried and powered; anti-inflammatory, antibacterial and high in antioxidants

Cocoa Powder - Brown color; for firm skin, improves blood flow

Coffee - Brown to Black color; fine ground or instant; an antioxidant, good for exfoliating and gets rid of odor

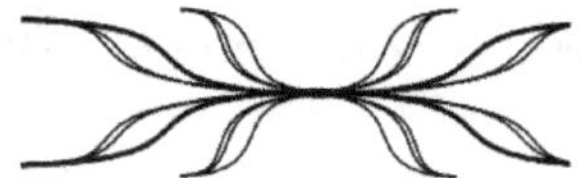

Simple Candle Making

The word "candle" means to glow, burn or shine.

Reeds, flax or cotton fibers placed into bowls of melted animal fat or tallow were lit, creating light within the darkness. This was the beginning of candles and candle making. Unfortunately, these first candles produced a bad smell as the fat burned. Over the years, many people began to look for an alternative that still gave a bright light but had a more pleasant smell.

Those who kept bees used the wax from the hives to create candles. The dried fluff from the stems and leaves of the Mullein plant were the wicks. Once they became popular, they also became expensive, and were made for lighting in the houses of the well-to-do for many years. The beeswax had a honey-like smell and created a brighter light.

Poorer populations in the cities and rural areas could not afford beeswax, and up until the 18th century, tallow candles were all they had for lighting. In the 1890s, a cheaper paraffin candle was introduced that burnt brighter and cleaner.

In 1991, soy candles became popular, as they left no residue.

Four kinds of wax you can use:

Old candles: The pieces are recycled. Simply melt them and remove old wicks.
Melting point: 185 degrees (85°C)

Beeswax candles are natural and freshly made ones still have a honey scent.
Melting point: 145 degrees (62.7°C)

Paraffin wax candles melt quickly, are cheap and easily scented or colored.
Melting point: 122 to 140°F (50 and 60°C)

Soy wax candles burn more slowly than other wax candles.
Melting point: 170 to 180 degrees (76.6 and 82.2°C)

Preparing the Candle

*** Put newspaper, wax paper, or rags down on the surface you are working on**. Fill a large stainless steel pot halfway with water and place it on the stove. When the water begins to boil, place a smaller pot or container inside the large pot. Cut up the wax into small chucks and place them into the smaller container to melt.

** **Note:** Do not place pot with wax directly on burner. It could catch fire. It could also evaporate.

*** Add scent and coloring before you pour off into candle molds.**

*** A mold can be anything that can withstand the temperature of the hot wax.**
Set a wick in the center of your candle mold. Lay a pencil, pen or small stick across the top of your mold. The wick (should be at least 2 inches from top of mold) can be wrapped around any of these to center it and keep it stable. Make sure the wick is straight, and the tip of wick is resting on the bottom of the mold.

*** Once you are set up, pour the wax slowly into the molds and set them in a level place where they can cool.** Note that if you are using beeswax, it may shrink a bit. Cooling period: 2 hours (old wax), 4-5 hours (soy), 6 hrs. (Beeswax) and 24 (paraffin).

Though some waxes cool faster than others, it is advised to let the candles rest for at least 24 hours. Trim finished wick down to ¼ inch.

****

Colored Candles and What They Represent:

The symbol of a light within the dark became part of many spiritual traditions. Colored candles lit with intent can help put into focus, the problem or idea that needs to be addressed. Note that if you cannot find the color you need, a white candle marked with the color needed or a specific colored ribbon tied onto the candle will work.

Red - Sex and passion, energy, blood and fertility, courage and anger (Mars energy)

These candles are used in workings for fertility and passion. A red candle is considered the "Mother" candle in the three phases of womanhood. Red candles are burned in spells for protection from psychic attack.

Pink – Love, female, romance, children, happiness

Pink candles are used in forgiveness and reconciliation spells.

Orange – Vitality, warmth and social activity; attracts positive changes (Jupiter energy)

Orange candles are used for health, job and creative art spells.

Yellow – Thought and intelligence; use of creativity and being optimistic (Sun energy)

Use yellow candles in spells for business workings.

Green – Money and prosperity, growth and healing; used in handfasting (Venus energy)

Used in luck drawing spells, green candles are burned to counteract jealousy and greed.

Blue – Focus, insight and loyalty (Uranus energy)

Dark Blue – Joy, laughter; overcoming depression (Saturn energy)

Light Blue – Compassion and caring, inspiration and serenity (Moon energy)

Light blue candles are burned for emotional healing spells.

Indigo Blue – Intuition, mental stability (Jupiter energy)

Purple – Power, wisdom, imagination and spirit; mystery and magic, protection and empowerment; jinx removal (Neptune energy)

Purple candles are burned as a focus in developing your psychic ability.

Lavender – Fantasy, dreams, balance and peace (Neptune and Venus energy)

Burn lavender candles for creativity.

Gold – Fast luck. Winnings (Sun energy)

Gold is burned as a God aspect in rituals.

Gray – Integration and mysticism; hex and spell reversals (Saturn energy)

Gray candles are used for integration spells.

Silver – Lunar rituals; astral energy. Psychic ability. Removes negative energies. (Moon energy)

Silver candles are burned to represent the Goddess in ritual work.

White – Symbol of the light, purity, innocence and revealing; protection (Moon energy)

White candles used in churches, spiritual and mystical institutions serve as a symbol of the light of revealing. A single candle in the darkness can represent hope to many people who have none. Many people light white candles with hopes of celebration or a wish for a loved one's return. A white candle represents a "Maiden" candle that is used in representing the three phases of womanhood.

Black – Symbol of the dark, hidden, authoritative (Pluto energy)

A black candle represents the "Crone" candle in the three phases of womanhood.

These candles are great for looking within. They can unblock things. Unveiling secrets; finding hidden things. Black candles can be used for protection spells as well.

Brown – Secure and grounded. Relates to the earth and its animals. (Mercury/Earth energy)

Brown candles are used mostly for the health and security of animals, wild or tamed. They are a good foundation and growth candle. They also work well with green candles for money spells.

Candles for each day of the week

These correspond to the five known planets along with the sun and moon.

Monday–White, silver or gray - Moon

Tuesday– Red - Mars

Wednesday– Purple - Mercury

Thursday– Blue - Jupiter

Friday– Green - Venus

Saturday– Purple or black - Saturn

Sunday– Yellow or gold candles – Sun

Honeybees

A fertile beehive in folk art tradition represents, unity, community and wealth.

Living in colonies of about 40,000, bees create their living space through "hive mind." This is a process where a collective of bees makes the choices for the construction and the survival of the hive. Each colony has three types of bees: the queen, the female workers and the male drones.

The female worker bees are normally sterile and the queen is the egg producer. Worker bees defend the hive, keep it cool and produce honey. The bees in the hive lick pheromones produced by the queen off her body as they pass her. These pheromones give the hive a state of wellbeing and indicate if the queen is healthy. If the old queen in a hive is dying or gone, a new queen needs to develop and hatch. Created by the workers, royal jelly is fed to a developing larva in the hive. This produces the queen bee. Two or more queens are created to insure survival. When hatched, the weaker queens are either killed in battle with another queen or are driven out of the hive.

The drones are male and do not have stingers. The only job the drones have is to fertilize the new queen in her maiden flight. A lack of drones in a colony could indicate poor food stores in the hive. The queen and drone mate in mid-air. A queen should mate with at least fifteen different drones in order to produce healthy eggs during her lifetime. She will produce around 2,000 to 2,500 eggs a day until her hive is filled.

After mating season in the fall, drones are pushed out of the hive to die. They have fulfilled their purpose. When winter comes, about half the colony will die out as well.

Honey

Honey starts out as nectar collected by worker bees from local flowers. This nectar is broken down into simple sugars which is then stored in a honeycomb. Liquid honey is produced when evaporation of these sugars occurs inside the honeycomb cell. Worker bees have been known to visit over two million flowers in order to produce enough nectar to make one pound of honey. Besides the amount ingested as food, a honeybee hive can produce about 65 pounds of surplus honey each year.

The flavors and colors of honey vary as to where the bees collect their nectar. Appalachian honey has a large variety of necture sources: alfalfa, apple blossom, aster, basswood, black locust, blackberry, buckwheat, Canadian thistle, clover, sweet clover, white clover, corn, dandelion, goldenrod, Japanese knotweed, milkweed, paulownia, prickly ash, pussy willow, red maple, redbud, Russian sage, sourwood, starhorn, sumac, sunflower, tree of heaven, tulip poplar, and witch hazel. Sourwood being the most popular in taste.

Beegums

Beegums are traditionally a three-foot piece of black gum tree hollowed out for hive use. Four holes are drilled into the trunk piece and two clean, stripped branches or dows, are placed in a cross shape through the holes at right angles. At the point where these two branches meet inside, a bee brood area can be started and is built downward. A piece of corn cob covered in honey is suspended from underneath the top of the lid, so the worker bees will produce the wax cells to store the honey. Honey can be removed by lifting the top slowly and cutting. This will not hurt the brooding chambers suspended below.

A different approach from this is to use a piece of the "bee tree." Beekeepers search for hives formed inside recently fallen trees that have no heavily developed rot. Beekeepers cut these to harvest honey or the colony itself. To find a "bee tree", beekeepers may follow a bee from its water source as bee trees are usually found not far from water. Go to a stream, creek or river and find a moist mossy, muddy or wet sandy spot. This is where bees usually drink. Once you see them, watch from which direction they are flying from discover where they came from. They usually fly a straight line from the hive. Walk around the area and you will soon find the tree. Once the downed tree is located and you find the point where the bees enter, cut the tree about four foot below and about three and a half foot above the hole.

Bee Lore

* If a bee touches a baby's lips, the child may become a great speaker or poet.

* If a bee flies through your house, it is a sign of good luck.

* Your luck will turn bad if you sell your bees.

* If someone gives you a hive with bees, you must in turn give honeycomb and honey to the giver.

* Do not swear at your bees; they will leave you and not come back.

* In the Christian faith, bees represent wisdom and resurrection.

* Bee hives are to be draped in black cloth when a member of the beekeeping family dies. This keeps the bees from leaving.

* When a beekeeper dies, it is a custom to invite his bees to the funeral and lay out food or drink for them.

* The bee and its hive are important symbols in Masonic and Freemason traditions symbolizing hard work and industry.

* If someone steals a hive, the bees within it will leave or die.

* If a bee lands on you, you will have great fortune in finances. If a bee lands on your hand, you will soon receive money.

* Scots in the Appalachians once believed that when they were asleep, their soul could leave their body in the shape of a bee or fly.

* Lovers walked by beehives to prove their faithfulness. Many believed the bees would know if someone was unfaithful in their relationship. Whoever was unfaithful would be stung.

* If you have to sell your bees, the money must be laid on a rock and cannot be picked up until the bees and their hives are long gone.

* **Swarm** in May worth a load of hay; Swarm in June worth a silver spoon; Swarm in July not worth a fly.

* **Bees** symbolize the sun and the harvest.

* **If** you do not move the hives when a family member dies, the bees will die or leave.

* **Honey** is the only food that contains all the essentials of life: Water, vitamins, minerals and enzymes.

* **The** personality of the hive is the same as the queen bee living in it. If the queen is aggressive, the hive is as well.

* **If** a bee flies into your house, you will have a visitor. If you kill a bee in your house, you will hear bad news.

* **Honey** bees were brought over to the northeastern United States in 1622 from England bound for the Virginia colony. It is said that natives there first called the bee, "White man's flies."

* **Bees** are the symbol of good luck and hard work.

* **Telling** your bees of family births and weddings brought good fortune to the family.

* **When** moving beehives, a beekeeper should leave out a dab of honey for the fairies.

* **Some** believe worker bees are pure. They are not known to produce many eggs and those they do produce, are either unfertilized or can produce drones. Only the queen produces fertilized eggs that hatch female worker bees. If the queen notices any of the worker bee's eggs, she will eat them.

* **A** folk remedy to relieve the pain of arthritis and rheumatism is bee stings.

Making Mountain Moonshine

In the still of the pre-dawn hours, the smell of sour mash filled the air.

A Wilkes County copper moonshine still
Courtesy of Appalachian Cultural Museum
Appalachian State University Boone, North
Carolina http://www.ibiblio.org/moonshine/make/make.html

E conomy in many struggling hill towns was destroyed during the 1930s Depression. Lumber and mining businesses were starting to use new mechanization techniques that left workers with fewer jobs. Bad farming practices and plant planning, stripped the soil and started producing poor crops for the farmers in local communities. Families who had homesteads in the mountains became extremely poverty-stricken.

Whiskey making had been common in the Appalachians' since the 1600s. Many families kept their own stills for home purposes. Without jobs, money and in some cases, food, the smuggling of homemade liquor became a necessity. Corn, ground into meal, was made into a mash from which alcohol was distilled. It was unbonded whiskey with nicknames such as shine, white lightning, panther-piss, corn liquor, mountain dew, forty-rod, corn squeezins and popskull.

Mountain farmers who grew corn or grain realized that they made very little by bushel (about .50) when they sold their grain for food or animal meal. This same amount of grain could be used to make white, unaged whiskey. Growers could make as much as $2.50 per bushel of grain when sold for the use of distilling liquor.

Distilled whiskey was more portable. The problem was that any alcohol at that time, was being heavily taxed and strict laws prohibiting the manufacturing of any liquor was in place. Prohibition banned the production of alcohol in the United States from 1920-33.

Prideful resistance to government authority was strong, as many of the poor mountain families felt the government did not help them when they were in true need. Their community (which supported them) was more important to them than the federal law. Many people in these small towns didn't mind running interference for a moonshiner when the federal marshals came looking for a local still.

Isolated areas were well protected against the "Revenuers." Places like Dark Corner in South Carolina became a dangerous area to pass through. **Appalachian history.net** writer David Tabler posted an excellent blog called, ***"You don't mean to go into the Dark Corner, do you?"*** about the towns of Landrum, Gowensville, and Glassy Mountain and their surrounding hillsides. The Dark Corner is located in the mountainous area of Greenville County and has a notorious history and violent reputation involving bootlegging. Here is an exerpt from Tabler's post:

"In setting out for the Dark Corner, I answered the warnings of my friends who said I would never return, by telling them that I would not only return, but I would bring back some moonshine, which seemed to be the foundation of the Dark Corner's evil repute. In order that I could keep my promise, the proprietor of the livery stable handed me two pint flasks, one of which was filled with yellow kernels of corn.

He explained the presence of the corn, in that whisky being very scarce since prohibition had gone into effect, someone had offered to fetch "a pint of good old corn: for fifty cents, and after getting the fifty cents, he had sent back the flask filled with the corn. It was not the kind of corn anticipated." (Tabler, 2016).

Many bootleggers illegally "running liquor" from the "Revenuers" were taking their loads of shine to Spartanburg and Greenville, South Carolina to keep the money flowing into the hills in order to buy food and other supplies for families there. The drivers drove vehicles that looked normal to avoid detection but beneath the surface they were "stocked" with high-powered engines for speed. Strong shocks where added as well to keep the liquor jars from breaking or spilling. Most of the cars had no backseat.

Bootlegging eventually stopped the attempts of the United States government from regulating taxation through the making of liquor. However, something else came from that situation as well. Still popular in many southern racing circuits, stock car and Nascar driving originated from these poor but proud hill folk who ran liquor to put food on the table and to avoid government penalties they felt were unfair.

How to Make Moonshine using the 10-10-10 method:

****Note: For informational purposes only****

* **10 gallons of water brought to a boil**

* **10 pounds of cornmeal is added.** Use a wooden paddle or large spoon and stir until the mixture becomes thick. Remove from heat, strain the grain off, pour in large plastic bucket to cool.

* **Stir 10 pounds of sugar into the wash.** Mix well.

* **When the wash (mixture) cools to 90 degrees, you will add ½ ounce of yeast.** Stir.

Pour it into a container and let it set for 8-10 days. Place it in a cool, dark place and cover the top with cheesecloth. This keeps the wash clean and allows the gases to escape as it ferments. Foam will eventually start to rise in the bucket. When it stops rising, yeast has eaten the sugar and produces alcohol. Distill.

The first couple of ounces is called "heads." This liquid should be discarded, or you can use it later as a cleaning agent. It contains acetone and ethanol. It is toxic and has a smell like finger nail polish remover.

The second part is where the good liquor is produced. It is called the body or "hearts" and has the most ethanol and is extracted when the liquid reaches 190-205 degrees. ** **Note: Anything collected before the proper temperature is methanol and other toxic waste products and should be discarded.**

The ending liquid is called "tails" and is cloudy and bitter. This can either be discarded or used in the next batch made.

To Distill: Strain mixture with strainer or cheesecloth and pour into a stainless steel container with tight lid. Slowly heat up. A copper coil connected at the top of the still will collect the steam as it evaporates. The copper coil or "worm "is threaded into a water barrel with a water intake and an outlet to keep cool water flowing through so that the steam in the coil will condense and drip into a distillation container.

Moonshine when done is between 180 and 190 proof and is pure grain. You can cut it to half strength by adding spring water.

A quick way to check the proof of your moonshine is to shake the jar it is in. If large bubbles form and disappear quickly, the alcohol content is high. If smaller bubbles form and disappear slowly, the alcohol content is lower.

Drinking moonshine can be dangerous. One of the ways to check for safety is to set a spoonful of the liquid on fire and watch for the color of the flame. Supposedly, if it burns with a blue flame, it is good whiskey. If it burns with a yellow flame, it is tainted. Car radiator coils have been known to be used as condensers, putting lead byproducts into the brew. It will burn with a red flame when lit if lead is present.

Just remember: **Yellow and Red** can make you dead.

Tracking: Animal Signs

Native peoples learned to track in order to locate, hunt and to understand the ways of animals.

A nimal tracks are imprints or marks made by the feet, tails, heads or antlers of animals on the surfaces they pass through. Just this small amount of information can reveal the animal's body size, basic shape, whether they were running or walking. Age and gender can be found the same way.

Locating signs or patterns of the animal's activity fills in more of the story. It could be a trail, left behind hair or fur, strong odors, nests or pallets of grass, leaves or branches, urine marks or scat, discarded food, broken tree branches, cuts or scratches on tree bark or chewed marks are called signs. Tracks and signs together are called spoor.

Environment and feeding behavior can tell you what types of animals may be present. A variety of plants for food and a good water source is a perfect environment for plant eaters, who have blunt teeth for grinding and chewing. Predators need to be present in order to keep these animal populations balanced and in control. If not, herbivores can overwhelm an area, stripping plant life away and destroying the environment.

An area that has herbivores sighted on them is a healthy environment for predators. These animals have pointed teeth for biting, claws for tearing and they stalk their prey. Check scat by breaking it apart to see what an animal has been eating in order to determine if it belongs to a plant eater or meat eater. A plant eater will have plants and seeds in their scat and a carnivore will have bones, hair or feathers mixed in.

Types of Prints:

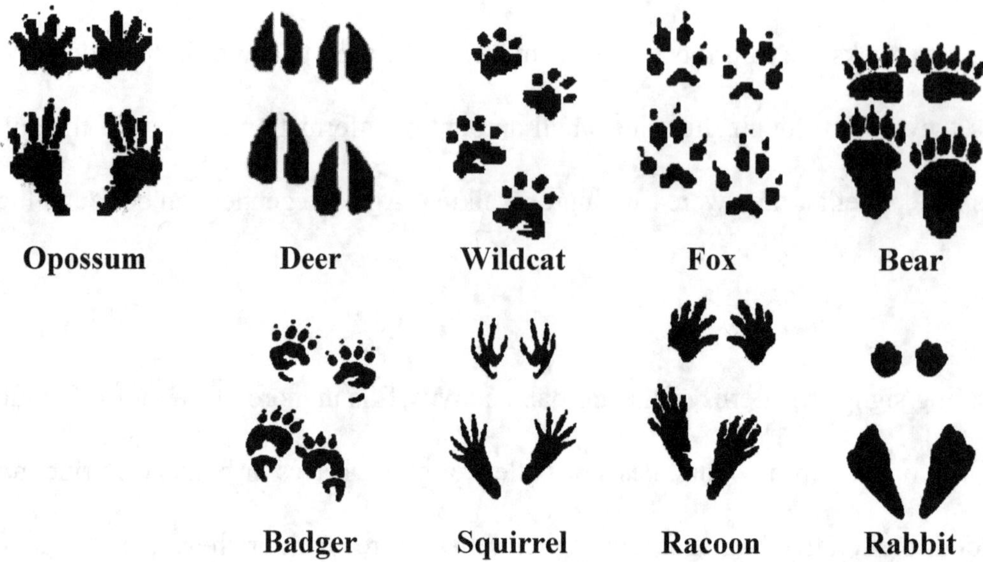

Opossum	Deer	Wildcat	Fox	Bear

Badger	Squirrel	Racoon	Rabbit

(Ursidae) Bear Family: With five toes and claw extensions, the bear's whole foot impression is similar to a human foot. They are not known to leave a distinct print unless it has snowed or there is wet ground. A typical track is an impression of the sole of the bear's foot with some toe or claw markings.

(Canidae) Canine Family: Main foot pad with four toes each and claw indentions. Most canines walk in what is called an "indirect register." That means that the back paws print falls behind and a bit to the side of the front paw print. The only exception in the Canine family of this kind of this type of movement is the fox. The fox walks in a "direct register", meaning that the fox's hind paws fall into the impressions of its forepaws. It is much like a cat's movement when it walks. Canine members: Dogs, coyotes, foxes and wolves.

(Felidae) Feline Family: Cats also have a main foot pad with four toes, but their toe pads are rounded and show no claw marks. This is due to their ability to retract their claws when walking. They walk in a "direct register", meaning that their hind paws fall into the impressions of their front feet as they walk. Feline members: House cats, bobcats, cougars and lynx

Horned Mammal Family: Heart shaped prints; single sided (half heart) or double sided (whole heart). Horned animals: deer, goats, sheep, caribou, musk ox, moose, elk and reindeer.

(Didelphidae) Opossum: The foot pad has five toes with claw indentions. The hind foot has an opposable thumb. This thumb lacks a claw and is noticeable in the impression. The front feet and the hind feet overlap each other in their tracks as they walk and can make the print bigger looking.

(Leporidae) Rabbit and Hare Family: Back feet are longer in print than front feet. Most of this family has four toes straight ahead both on the front and hind legs.

Related to…

(Ochotonidae) Marsh hare and pika: These mammals have four slender toes with claw indentions and a back pad.

(Procyonidae) Raccoon: The front and hind foot pads both have five toes with claw indentions. Front feet resemble small human hands and the hind legs have a longer heel and look like human feet. They walk flat-footed.

(Rodentia) Rodent Family: Four toe prints with claw extensions in the front and five on the hind legs. Beavers and other larger rodent tracks have five toe prints in front legs and five in hind legs. Back leg tracks will be side by side, but front leg tracks are uneven. Some varieties, such as beavers, nutria and moles are webbed, because of their aquatic lifestyle. Rodent members: Mice, rats, squirrels, muskrats, chipmunks, gophers, voles, porcupines and beavers.

(Mustelidae) Weasel family: Five toes on front and back legs with sharp claw extensions. Somewhat inverted triangle or V shaped paw pad. Weasel members: Skunks, otters, ferrets, badgers, wolverines, minks, weasels, martens and fishers.

Scat
(excreted waste)

Carnivores: (example: cougar, lynx or bobcat) - Meat-eaters scat is long and has segmented sections. Fur, feathers, or small bones may be found in it.

Herbivores: (example: deer, goats or rabbits) - After eating vegetation, they excrete pellets.

Omnivores: (example: raccoon, black bear or coyote) - Scat is long and varied according to what they have eaten. You may find berries and bones in one piece of scat. The diameter of scat can tell the size of an animal and sometimes what species.

Tracking Tips

* **Y**ou can also determine whether an animal is male or female, especially in deer. In all animals, the bone structure is different in males as compared to females. A buck has broader shoulders and narrower hips and usually travels alone. Female deer usually put their back hoof off to the side when walking because of their broader hips and are usually in a group. Pregnant does walk forward on their front legs but have angle off to the side with both back legs. They usually carry two fawns when pregnant. Any deer tracks with smaller hoofs impressed on top, indicates that their herd has young ones traveling with them.

* Use all of your senses when tracking. Different types of animals have distinctly pungent scent glands or really strong urine. This is often used for defense, mating or marking territory.

* **A** den of copperheads smells like cucumbers.

* **W**ild pig urine has high ammonia content and a strong smell.

* **B**eavers smell like vanilla. They have a gland called castor sacs under the tail that produces a gooey substance that they use to mark their territory.

* **H**ow high a gnawed area on a tree can indicate the size of the animal that made it, be it on two legs or four.

* **S**igns of passage can include: tracks, signs of feeding, droppings, urine, hair, bones, feathers, chewed or broken vegetation, burrows, dens or nests, chewed nuts or seeds, stripped logs, scratching on bark or ground, wallows, holes in the ground or in the trees and signs of rubbings and broken or chewed tree limbs.

* **P**orcupine urine smells like pine trees. They eat pine needles, seeds and some of the inner bark of the tree.

* **S**igns that a predator approaches and area: birds are in trees and not on the ground. The lack of bird and insect song can indicate predators in the area.

* **B**ears rub themselves on the animals they kill or any other things they eat, in order to mask their smell. Some say their normal smell is a musky (when breeding); dirty wet dog smell.

* **B**y observing grasses and other greenery, you can tell what kind of animals has chewed on it. A clean diagonal cut in the bite could mean that rabbits or rodents have eaten there. Hoofed animals clamp down and pull upward, leaving a jagged cut. Canines or felines chew.

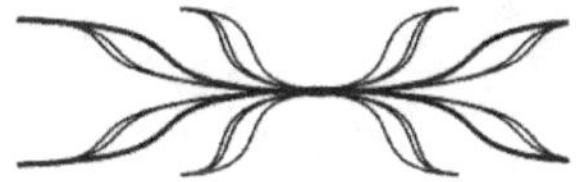

Spirit Guides: Animals

Tribal and spiritual totems show sides of human personality too.

Many Native Americans believe that all people have an animal alter-ego that helps develop their physical, emotional and spiritual personalities. These animal spirits are traditionally assigned to a native child either at birth or during the child's rite of passage into adulthood. They could be animals first seen or animals that stand out and seemed to be giving a message to the seeker. Some are known be the givers of prophecy in their unusual white-colored or albino form, such as a white buffalo. The medicines these animals can teach us help overcome weaknesses or show ways of strength or survival. Native clans have been known to live a lifestyle according to their animal's totem; believing that in times of great stress, they can transform into their totem animal and spiritually travel in order to find the answers they seek.

Native shamans have been known to "share" themselves, through spiritual ritual, with an animal in order to see through the animal's eyes and have a spiritual revealing. Animal totems made of stone and wood, relate to major native family bloodlines. Each family line carries specific qualities of strength, courage or wisdom, much like the animal spirits that are represented in their carvings.

1888- Swimmer, the Cherokee cultural preservationist, storyteller and shaman
Smithsonian Institution, Public Domain

The belief in animal spirits has spread through generations of hill people too, and many living in the wilderness found signs and symbols that were important for survival. As more and more people connected to the native spiritual beliefs, folk tales became known of the very human nature of our animal brothers and their adventures. Their stories were learning tools for the mountain culture's lifestyle. Many people still watch each day for signs. Animal spirit messages are most noted by people living in rural areas. Below is a list of animals that live in or around the Appalachian Mountains, foothills or marshland areas and what their animal spirit represents.

Animal Spirit Qualities

Alligator - Fierceness, survival, primordial

Badger - Aggressive, fighter, territorial, war-like

Bat - Sonar, rebirth, instinct, intuition, inner journey

Bear - Called the great healer by Native Americans. When wounded, they find and use herbs to heal their bodies. They are symbols of strength and courage.

Beaver - Industrious, hard-working, engineers, wood workers, builders

Boar - Power, aggression, fearless, survival

Bobcat - Stealth; the ability to adapt and survive. Clear vision.

Buffalo - Sacred, White Buffalo Woman, blessing, strength, gratitude, grounding, primal

Bull - Fertility, strength, territorial, bluntness, willfulness, power

Cat - Stealth, mystery, hidden, independence, magic, guardian

Cougar - Watchful, aware, leaders, courage

Cow - Docile, content, home loving

Coyote - Trickery, sneaky, stealth, guile, planner, shape-shifting

Deer - Graceful, gentle, innocence, peaceful, compassionate

Dog - Protective, loyal, faithful, guidance

Elk - Strength, endurance, raw power, wisdom, fertility

Falcon - Messengers, prophecy, guardian, leader, going against the odds, hunter

Fish - Good luck, transformation, magic, fertility, emotional message, rebirth

Fox - Wild and cunning, shapeshifter, negotiator, intelligent, crafty

Frog - Cleansing, rebirth, water, medicine worker, transforming

Goat - Stubborn, upward-climbing, earth, endurance

Horse - Power, endurance, nobility, journey, stamina, travel and freedom

Lizard - Perspective, hidden, planning, cold blooded, vision, changes

Lynx - Secretive, hunter, quiet, planner, unconventional, awareness

Mole - Sensitive, hidden, searcher, underground/underworld message, seeker in the darkness

Moose - Strength, dignity, fortitude, endurance, headstrong/stubborn, wisdom

Mouse - Scrutiny, organization, energy, locators, fine details, nest builder

Opossum - Misdirection, passive-aggressive, clever

Otter - Playful, clever, intelligent, family orientated

Ox - Faith, strong, enduring, plodding, strong hearted, sacrifice

Panther - Silence, hunter, stealth, introspection, night vision, caution, strength

Porcupine - Shy, withdrawn, prickly, curious, innocence

Rabbit - Curiosity, fear, fertility, lunar magic

Raccoon - Stealth, intelligence, scavenger, washer

Ram - Willful, deliberate, stubborn, challenging, powerful

Rat - Aggressive, intelligent, quick thinking, scavengers

Salamander - Passion and luck

Scorpion - Hidden dangers; aggression

Skunk - Reputation, respect, strength

Snake - Wisdom, transforming, rebirth, enemy to some, strikes quickly, sexuality

Squirrel - Worker, talker, gatherer, social, playful, digger

Stag - Ruler, protector, rebirth, guardian, royal, enduring

Toad - Prophecy and visions, transformation, intention

Turtle - Carrier of the Earth, long lived, slow moving, patience, endurance

Weasel - Sneaky, devious, aggressive, wild

Wolf - Freedom, loner, teacher, hunter, loyal to pack

****

Bird Spirits and Symbolism

Blackbird - Knowledge and wit

Bluebird - Happiness and hope

Blue jay - Faithfulness, truth and loyalty

Cardinal - Joy and celebration

Catbird - Language and communication

Chickadee - Speaker of the truth; knowledge

Crane - Long life, intelligence, independence

Crow - shape-shifter, darkness, endings, magic, watchful, creator, messengers

Cuckoo - Deception; infidelity

Dove - Spirit, peace, love, messengers, sight

Duck - The ability to float on top of things, water energy, family

Eagle - Courage, Great Spirit, independence, flight and soar, fighter, freedom

Egret - Prosperity and good fortune

Finch - Happiness and celebration

Goldfinch - Enthusiasm; finding joy in the moment

Goose - Vigilant, demanding, productive, guardian, valor, loyalty and devotion

Grackle - The use of mind and heart

Grouse - Spiral dance, connection to the sky and earth, personal power

Hawk - Noble, visionary, guardian, messenger, hunter, victory in battle

Heron - Independent, self-reliant, fishing, balanced, purity, patience and long life

Heron - Kingfisher - Peace and prosperity and good fortune

Hummingbird - Joy, quickness, communication, warrior, energy, messenger

Loon - Earth-Diver; tranquility & serenity

Nightingale - Love and longing

Owl - Wisdom, seer, magic, death, message, vision, night hunter

Peacock - Pride, sexuality, self-esteem, beauty, sight

Pheasant – Creativity, love

Pigeon – Sacrifice, love and peace

Quail - Protector of children, messages

Raven - Mystical, transforming, scavenger, intelligent, prophetic messages, dark/light, vision; "rain crow"

Robin - Renewal, passion, birth, honor

Rooster - Announcer, aggressive, protective, leader

Scarlet Tanager -Warmth and brightness

Sparrow - Simplicity and hard work

Starling - Communication and dreams; visions

Swallow - Everlasting love, loyalty

Swan - Grace, beauty, movement, dreams, purity

Swift - Agility and speed

Thrush - Insight and freedom

Towhee - Persistence, revealing truth

Turkey - Great giver, blessings, abundance

Turkey Buzzard - Cleansing and transformation

Warbler - Voice; communication, song

Woodpecker - Messenger, determination, balanced, controlled

Wren - Alertness, vibrancy

Insects of Myth and Legend - What each represents and spirit work

Ant - Hard worker; the ability to overcome problems, teamwork

Beetle – Protection, messenger, change and regeneration

Bee - Producers, organization, message bearer, messenger between this world and the spirit, wisdom, sweetness

Butterfly - The soul. A major change comes into your life. Metamorphosis. Grace.

Caterpillar - Transition and change

Cicada - Cycles, slow growth

Cricket - A singer of songs, announcement and warning

Cockroach - Scavenger

Firefly - Light bringer, code talker

Fly - Observation and persistence

Damselfly - Warrior

Dragonfly - Transformation, true vision, crosser of worlds

Grasshopper - Free spirit, lucky

Ladybug - Home and family

Mosquito – Persistence, blood magic

Moth - Lunar energy; illusion

Praying Mantis – Assassin, stillness

Spider - Weaver, collector of dreams (Grandmother Spider Woman), planner of fate, protection, trapper

Snail - Slow and steady

Tick - Blood sucker, collector

Wasp - Soldier, warnings

Worm - Keeper of the ground and tunnels

The Language of Trees and Spiritual Attributes in the Appalachians

Apple - Virtue and motherhood

Apricot - Distrust and doubt

Ash - Sacrifice and high awareness

Aspen - Determination and clarity of purpose

Beech - Tolerance

Birch - Truth and new beginnings

Cedar - Protection and prosperity

Cherry - Rebirth and compassion

Crabapple - Love, marriage and fertility

Cypress - Death and immortality

Chestnut - Harvest, overcoming difficulties and chastity

Dogwood - Strength, protection and will

Elm - Wisdom and will

Fir - Honesty, truth and strength

Fig - Luxury, fertility and sweetness

Hawthorn - Love and protection

Hemlock - Sacred tree of protection and healing

Hickory - Flexibility and balance

Hornbeam - Muscle wood, boundaries, protection

Laurel - Victory and recognition

Linden - Friendship and loyalty

Locust - God's judgment, destruction

Magnolia - Dignity and nobility

Maple - Offerings and promise

Mimosa - Sensitivity

Mulberry - Faith and transformation

Oak - Courage and strength

Peach - Marriage, rebirth and immortality

Pear - Lust and love

Pecan - Higher awareness, work and money

Persimmon - Love, fertility and knowledge

Pine - Peace and creativity

Plum - Good fortune, happiness and beauty

Rowen - Tree of life

Spruce - Boldness, faithfulness

Sycamore - Ambition and clarity

Tulip Popular - Grounding, security and independence

Willow - Inner wisdom, age

Walnut - True focus, energy

White Pine - Serenity; peacemaker

Yew - Death and rebirth

Powwow, Hoodoo, Serpents, Prayer and Folk Healing

A folk religion (Dutch-German) brought to the mountains by settlers that use healings, charms and prayer. **"Powwowing"** uses many types of healing rituals for treating ailments in people and animals. Practitioners (a Powwow man or woman) use these rituals to help others in physical and spiritual protection, as well as good luck.

Mountain Powwow Tradition

The belief in Powwow came into the Appalachian mountain regions by the Pennsylvania Dutch or German settlers. Passed on from male to female and from female to male in family lines, the gift of healing can be traced back hundreds of years, and the use of prayer, conjure, herbals, healing charms and root working have been their tools. If one of these practitioners should ever come to your door and help you with a problem, **do not thank them. Instead, bless them with a gift for services rendered.**

The use of the Christian bible is important to their work, and its verses are used to create a type of sympathetic magic that links faith with healing. An example of this would be the reciting of a bible verse, such as Ezekiel 16:6 the King James Version

The Body of Christ and the Staunching of Blood

"And when I passed by thee, and saw thee polluted in thine own blood, I said unto thee *when thou wast* in thy blood, Live; yea, I said unto thee *when thou wast* in thy blood, Live." (KJB)

This prayer is used during a ceremony to staunch blood. The Powwow person presses their hands on the wound, and the prayer is said. Signs of the cross are made over the area. The healer then commands the blood to stop flowing in the name of God the Father, God the Son, and God the Holy Ghost, Amen.

** Some believe the ability to stop blood flow in a wound can only be conducted by a witch doctor/medicine man or woman of the opposite sex.

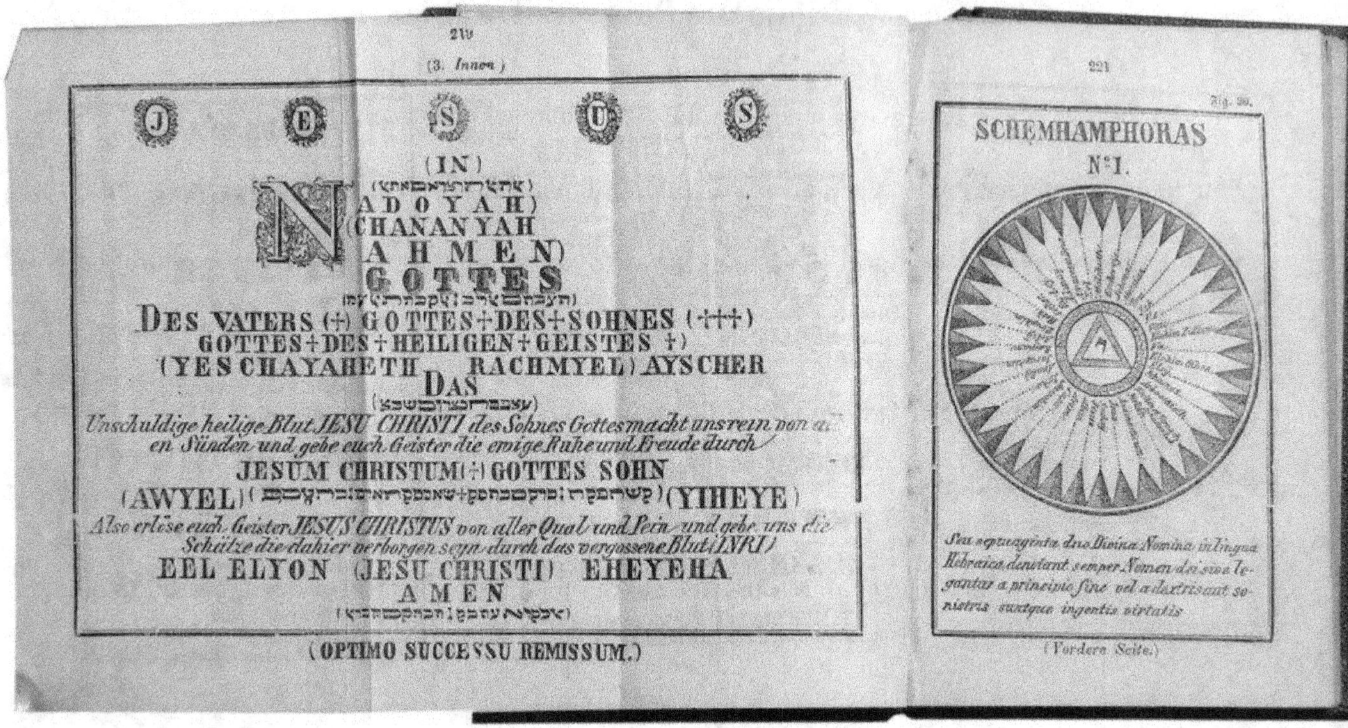

From: Powwowing in Pennsylvania: Healing Rituals of the Dutch Country - Glencairn Museum
https://goo.gl/images/QaVWhz
The Sixth and Seventh Books of Moses

John George Hohman's book *Pow-Wows or Long Lost Friend* has what he called, "A remedy to stop bleeding." (Hohman 1820) The person bleeding must be addressed by their full name as the healer requests that the blood slow and stop. He then says this prayer:

"Jesus Christ dearest blood!

That stoppeth the pain and stoppeth the blood.

In this help you (person's name)

God the Father, God the Son, God the Holy Ghost. Amen."

Here is one to relieve a headache:
(Repeat three times, allowing three minutes between each saying)

"Tame thou flesh and bone, like Christ in paradise; and who will assist thee, this I tell

thee (name) for your repentance-sake."

Talking Fire Out of Burns

Mary Martin's grandfather rushed to her aid when she burned the palm of her hand on the stove. After running her hand under some cold water from the tap, the fiery red area began to spread across her palm. Seeing this, her grandfather had Mary sit down at the kitchen table. As he sat at the table with her, he calmed her down by talking softly and assuring her all would be fine. Then, holding her hand in his, he began to blow on the burn and asked the fire to leave Mary's hand. He prayed over the wound reciting quotes from the bible. After a while, he wrapped the burn in clean gauze. When Mary went to bed that night, she noticed the burn was no longer hurting, and when she unwrapped the wound, the skin was turning a healing pink.

Soothing a Teething Baby

Rubbing a little vanilla on the baby's gums and placing some yarrow sprigs above and at the bottom of the baby's bed, the healer then takes a silver dime that belonged to him from his pocket and gives it to the baby's father. The father (or grandfather) punches a hole in the center of the coin and sands it smooth around the edges. Then a thin string (for around the neck) or a red ribbon (to hang over the cradle or crib) is threaded through the center to wear or to hang up.

Making crosses + + over the baby's crib, the healer might recite:

(Proverbs 3:5-6)
"Trust in the LORD with all thine heart; and lean not unto thine own understanding.
In all thy ways acknowledge him, and he shall direct thy paths."

Then the healer will make a request for healing; something like this:

"Lord, (baby's name) is in pain and needs your help. If you could just look down upon
her and bless her. Drive out the fear, and comfort (baby's name) through his/her pain.
In the name of God the Father, God the Son, and God the Holy Ghost, Amen. + + +"

As the child hopefully quiets, its pain easing off, the last prayer is said:

> **(Luke 11:1-4) "And it came to pass, that, as he was praying in a certain place, when he ceased, one of his disciples said unto him, Lord, teach us to pray, as John also taught his disciples.**
>
> **And he said unto them, when ye pray, say, Our Father which art in heaven, hallowed be thy name. Thy kingdom come. Thy will be done, as in heaven, so in earth.**
>
> **Give us day by day our daily bread.**
>
> **And forgive us our sins; for we also forgive every one that is indebted to us. And lead us not into temptation; but deliver us from evil." (KJB)**

Removing Warts

If you have warts, one of the more traditional mountain ways to cure it, was to steal a new potato and a dishtowel from your mother. Cutting the potato in half, you would then rub both sides of the potato on the wart, and then wrap it in the dishtowel. When the moon is full, bury the towel with the potato under your front stairs. You may have to repeat this process if your mother catches you stealing!

It is believed that you can "talk off a wart", while rubbing a penny on it.

Make a deep scratch or notch in a stick for each wart, then bury the stick and walk away. The warts should start to fade.

It's said that you can cure warts if someone buys them off you.

Roast chicken feet and then rub them on the wart. Bury them around the eaves of your house. Your wart will soon disappear.

Go to a rotten oak stump two or three days after a hard rain. Look for one that has water standing in it. Soak a rag in the stump water and wrap it over the wart as a bandage. Repeat. After a few days, the wart should fall off.

Take a piece of chicken gizzard and rub it on the wart. Bury the gizzard under a rock and as it rots, your wart will disappear.

Here is a particularly nasty one: While watching a funeral procession as it goes by, rub your wart and say, "Wart, wart, follow the corpse." The wart will eventually disappear from you and appear on the deceased person that is to be buried.

Sealing a Working

When you are finished with any kind of Powwow working, seal your work with the sign of the cross using your right hand. Make a fist and point your thumb up drawing it over the affected area in the name of the Father, Son and Holy Spirit. Do this three times.

Powwow and Death

It was not until the 1860s in the United States that professional funeral parlors were created. Older mountain houses were built with two doors in the front of the house. One door was the entrance to the living room where the "living" family and friends entered. The door beside it was known as the "funeral door" (usually connected to the parlor or another family room) where the dead family member was laid in state. Once the viewing was over, the deceased was taken out in their casket, feet-first through the door to be buried. (Coming in by birth, going out by death…).

When a person dies, either a Granny woman or the family members would wash, dress or wrap the body. Silver coins are placed on the eyes of the deceased to help keep them closed. Traditionally, these coins are considered payment to pay your way into heaven or to get the Ferryman to help the spirit cross over into the underworld.

The windows would be open (no air conditioning) and body would then lie in state from the time of death until the next day. Some try to keep the body for three days but usually the rot and smell forced the family to bury the body. Friends and family sat up with the dead. Originally, this tradition was created since ancient times to keep animals from making off with the body. Families also wanted to make sure the person in the casket was not still alive.

Those who visited brought food for the family, and for the night before the morning burial. A piece of bread was either placed in the dead person's hands, or a plate of food is placed on the top of the casket. The congregation would then wait for a man most people shunned except during funerals. He is called a "sin-eater." A **sin-eater** is a person who receive money to consume the ritual meal to magically take on the sins of the dead or dying.

Towards the end of the evening before burial, if invited by the family, a powwow medicine man may come in and place a broom by the funeral door to keep away malicious people and spirits. Lighting a bowl of herbs (parsley, basil or rosemary), the man will walk to all four corners of the room, filling the room with scent before putting the bowl to the side. Then, starting at the head of the deceased, he then walks clockwise around the casket three times, knocking on the floor with a cane and repeating: **"In repentance and rest is your salvation, in quietness and trust is your strength." (Isaiah 30:15)** This ritual is used to keep the dead's spirit calm and at peace, so it can be laid to rest.

People in mountain communities came together to help build the coffin and dig the grave. If a person died in the winter, a bonfire was built on the burial plot to thaw the ground, so the grave could be dug. If the grave could not be dug, the coffin with the body was placed in a barn or shed until spring. Burials usually took place at family homesteads.

Needing Help with a Snake Problem

****Note: The characters in this story are fictitious; the snake catcher's techniques are not. ****

Ed Reid noticed the feathers first. The summer breeze had blown them up from under his porch, and he recognized the speckled pattern on the feathers as belonging to one of his best laying hens. He hadn't seen her in three or four days and thought she had been randomly eaten by a fox. But it was worse than that; he discovered, he had one or more snakes living up under his house. He saw the head of one of the serpents pop out of a hole that morning beneath the porch. He thought something was a little odd when the chickens started to avoid his cabin, even with feed thrown outside. He sighed and shook his head. Reid was going to need a little help.

Calling Mark Redman was not easy. Catching him was the problem, as this is the season that he would be especially busy, and he had no answering machine connected to his house phone. Redman was known as a cunning man who was good at chasing away snakes from houses and barns. Reid was finally able to catch up with him that evening on the phone. Redman told Reid he would be by around ten o'clock the next morning.

Redman was a small man with a grizzled beard, which came down to the middle of his chest. He was dressed in a pair of faded bib-overalls and his pants were tucked into his work boots. A baseball cap covered his shaggy hair. He carried with him a heavy, wooden walking stick, and a bag was tied onto his belt. A small bible was sticking out of his back pocket.

Redman walked around Reid's house a couple of times, noting the snake holes and looking through the underpinned doors into the dark, moist areas of the crawlspace under the house. Returning to the front porch, he took the bag off his belt, and withdrew a small bottle of liquid and a large ball of hair. The ammonia smell was strong as he rubbed his work boots and his pants up to his knees. He then soaked some of the liquid onto the rags Reid had given him from the house, and folded pieces of hair into the cloth. He asked Reid to join him in prayer, saying he needed the Holy Spirit to be witness. Retying the bag to his belt, he took the rags and threw them under different parts of the crawlspace through the entrance doors. Then, starting from the back of the house, the cunning man proceeded to pound the staff loudly on the ground as he walked around the base of the house, "calling" the snakes out. He went slowly around the house three times. Fifteen minutes later, Reid watched on the front porch as a snake (looked like a copperhead) crawled out of the front crawlspace door and headed toward the woods; he saw another one on the grass nearby heading for a rocky outcrop.

After about another thirty minutes, Redman joined Reid on the porch where the cunning man received a paper bag with two dozen eggs and a ten-dollar bill. No words were said. Smiling, Redman waved his hat as he walked away.

****

Speaking of snakes, the shed skin of a snake can be used as powerful repellent. Dried and ground, this "snake dust" is used to repel mice and rats. This is usually placed in small cloth bags sewn with cotton thread, along with some red pepper or lavender. By the end of summer or the beginning of fall, scatter the bags in places rodents would be interested in visiting in the house. Used in a magical working, the powdered shed can be mixed with salt or herbs to repel unwanted people, too.

All parts of a snake are utilized when doing workings. A rattlesnake rattle is very powerful for sex or luck. Worn on a necklace, it is used for sexual attraction or carried it in a pocket, as a talisman. Gamblers use it along with a whole piece of High John root in a mojo or medicine bag for luck in gambling.

Mountain musicians placed rattlesnake rattles inside their guitars or fiddles. Not only would it keep animals from nesting inside the instruments, but many musicians believe it makes the music sound better and attract a bigger crowd of people that wanted to listen.

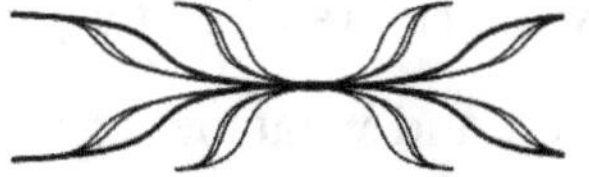

Psalms Used for Healing and Protection

Psalm 1:1-6 - For safe pregnancy (KJB)

"Blessed is the man that walketh not in the counsel of the ungodly, nor standeth in the way of sinners, nor sitteth in the seat of the scornful.

But his delight is in the law of the LORD; and in his law doth he meditates day and night.

And he shall be like a tree planted by the rivers of water, that bringeth forth his fruit in his season; his leaf also shall not wither; and whatsoever he doeth shall prosper.

The ungodly are not so: but are like the chaff which the wind driveth away.

Therefore, the ungodly shall not stand in the judgment, nor sinners in the congregation of the righteous.

The LORD knoweth the way of the righteous: but the way of the ungodly shall perish."

Psalm 7:1-17- Court cases; protection against the enemy (KJB)

" O Lord my God, in thee do I put my trust: save me from all them that persecute me, and deliver me: Lest he tear my soul like a lion, rending it in pieces, while there is none to deliver.

O LORD my God, if I have done this; if there be iniquity in my hands;
If I have rewarded evil unto him that was at peace with me; (yea, I have delivered him that without cause is mine enemy:) Let the enemy persecute my soul, and take it; yea, let him tread down my life upon the earth, and lay mine honour in the dust. Selah.

Arise, O LORD, in thine anger, lift up thyself because of the rage of mine enemies: and awake for me to the judgment that thou hast commanded.

So shall the congregation of the people compass thee about: for their sakes therefore return thou on high.

The LORD shall judge the people: judge me, O LORD, according to my righteousness, and according to mine integrity that is in me

Oh let the wickedness of the wicked come to an end; but establish the just: for the righteous God trieth the hearts and reins.

My defense is of God, which saveth the upright in heart.

God judgeth the righteous, and God is angry with the wicked every day.

If he turn not, he will whet his sword; he hath bent his bow, and made it ready.

He hath also prepared for him the instruments of death; he ordaineth his arrows against the persecutors.

Behold, he travaileth with iniquity, and hath conceived mischief, and brought forth falsehood.

He made a pit, and digged it, and is fallen into the ditch which he made.

His mischief shall return upon his own head, and his violent dealing shall come down upon his own pate.
will praise the LORD according to his righteousness: and will sing praise to the name of the LORD most high."

Psalm 10: 1-18 - To cleanse unclean spirits (KJB)

"Why standest thou afar off, O LORD? why hidest thou thyself in times of trouble?

The wicked in his pride doth persecute the poor: let them be taken in the devices that they have imagined.

For the wicked boasteth of his heart's desire, and blesseth the covetous, whom the LORD abhorreth.

The wicked, through the pride of his countenance, will not seek after God: God is not in all his thoughts.

His ways are always grievous; thy judgments are far above out of his sight: as for all his enemies, he puffeth at them.

He hath said in his heart, I shall not be moved: for I shall never be in adversity.

His mouth is full of cursing and deceit and fraud: under his tongue is mischief and vanity.

He sitteth in the lurking places of the villages: in the secret places doth he murder the innocent: his eyes are privily set against the poor.

He lieth in wait secretly as a lion in his den: he lieth in wait to catch the poor: he doth catch the poor, when he draweth him into his net.

He croucheth, and humbleth himself, that the poor may fall by his strong ones.

He hath said in his heart, God hath forgotten: he hideth his face; he will never see it.

Arise, O LORD; O God, lift up thine hand: forget not the humble.

Wherefore doth the wicked contemn God? he hath said in his heart, Thou wilt not require it.

Thou hast seen it; for thou beholdest mischief and spite, to requite it with thy hand: the poor committeth himself unto thee; thou art the helper of the fatherless.

Break thou the arm of the wicked and the evil man: seek out his wickedness till thou find none.

The LORD is King for ever and ever: the heathen are perished out of his land.

LORD, thou hast heard the desire of the humble: thou wilt prepare their heart, thou wilt cause thine ear to hear:
To judge the fatherless and the oppressed, that the man of the earth may no more oppress."

Psalm 18:1- 50 - Anointing and protection against strong enemies

"I will love thee, O LORD, my strength.

The LORD is my rock, and my fortress, and my deliverer; my God, my strength, in whom I will trust; my buckler, and the horn of my salvation, and my high tower.

I will call upon the LORD, who is worthy to be praised: so, shall I be saved from mine enemies.

The sorrows of death compassed me, and the floods of ungodly men made me afraid.

The sorrows of hell compassed me about: the snares of death prevented me.

In my distress I called upon the LORD AND cried unto my God: he heard my voice out of his temple, and my cry came before him, even into his ears.

Then the earth shook and trembled; the foundations also of the hills moved and were shaken, because he was wroth.

There went up a smoke out of his nostrils, and fire out of his mouth devoured: coals were kindled by it.

He bowed the heavens also and came down: and darkness was under his feet.

And he rode upon a cherub, and did fly: yea, he did fly upon the wings of the wind.

He made darkness his secret place; his pavilion round about him were dark waters and thick clouds of the skies.

At the brightness that was before him his thick clouds passed, hail stones and coals of fire.

The LORD also thundered in the heavens, and the Highest gave his voice; hail stones and coals of fire.

Yea, he sent out his arrows, and scattered them; and he shot out lightnings, and discomfited them.

Then the channels of waters were seen, and the foundations of the world were discovered at thy rebuke, O LORD, at the blast of the breath of thy nostrils.

He sent from above, he took me, he drew me out of many waters.

He delivered me from my strong enemy, and from them which hated me: for they were too strong for me.

They prevented me in the day of my calamity: but the LORD was my stay.

He brought me forth also into a large place; he delivered me, because he delighted in me.

The LORD rewarded me according to my righteousness; according to the cleanness of my hands hath he recompensed me.

For I have kept the ways of the LORD AND have not wickedly departed from my God.

For all his judgments were before me, and I did not put away his statutes from me.

I was also upright before him, and I kept myself from mine iniquity.

Therefore, hath the LORD recompensed me according to my righteousness, according to the cleanness of my hands in his eyesight.

With the merciful thou wilt shew thyself merciful; with an upright man thou wilt shew thyself upright;

With the pure thou wilt shew thyself pure; and with the froward thou wilt shew thyself froward.

For thou wilt save the afflicted people; but wilt bring down high looks.

For thou wilt light my candle: the LORD my God will enlighten my darkness.

For by thee I have run through a troop; and by my God have I leaped over a wall.

As for God, his way is perfect: the word of the LORD is tried: he is a buckler to all those that trust in him.1 For who is God save the LORD? or who is a rock save our God?

It is God that girdeth me with strength, and maketh my way perfect.

He maketh my feet like hinds' feet, and setteth me upon my high places.

He teacheth my hands to war, so that a bow of steel is broken by mine arms.

Thou hast also given me the shield of thy salvation: and thy right hand hath holden me up, and thy gentleness hath made me great.

Thou hast enlarged my steps under me, that my feet did not slip.

I have pursued mine enemies and overtaken them: neither did I turn again till they were consumed.

I have wounded them that they were not able to rise: they are fallen under my feet.

For thou hast girded me with strength unto the battle: thou hast subdued under me those that rose up against me.

Thou hast also given me the necks of mine enemies; that I might destroy them that hate me.

They cried, but there was none to save them: even unto the LORD, but he answered them not.

Then did I beat them small as the dust before the wind: I did cast them out as the dirt in the streets.

Thou hast delivered me from the strivings of the people; and thou hast made me the head of the heathen: a people whom I have not known shall serve me.

As soon as they hear of me, they shall obey me: the strangers shall submit themselves unto me.

The strangers shall fade away and be afraid out of their close places.

The LORD liveth; and blessed be my rock; and let the God of my salvation be exalted.

It is God that avengeth me, and subdueth the people under me.

He delivereth me from mine enemies: yea, thou liftest me up above those that rise up against me: thou hast delivered me from the violent man.

Therefore, will I give thanks unto thee, O LORD, among the heathen, and sing praises unto thy name.

Great deliverance giveth he to his king; and sheweth mercy to his anointed, to David, and to his seed for evermore.

Psalm 35: 1-28 – Winning legal fights and lawsuits (KJB)

"Plead my cause, O LORD, with them that strive with me: fight against them that fight against me.

Take hold of shield and buckler and stand up for mine help.

Draw out also the spear and stop the way against them that persecute me: say unto my soul, I am thy salvation.

Let them be confounded and put to shame that seek after my soul: let them be turned back and brought to confusion that devise my hurt.

Let them be as chaff before the wind: and let the angel of the LORD chase them.

Let their way be dark and slippery: and let the angel of the LORD persecute them.

For without cause have they hid for me their net in a pit, which without cause they have digged for my soul.

Let destruction come upon him at unawares; and let his net that he hath hid catch himself: into that very destruction let him fall.

And my soul shall be joyful in the LORD: it shall rejoice in his salvation.

All my bones shall say, LORD, who is like unto thee, which deliverest the poor from him that is too strong for him, yea, the poor and the needy from him that spoileth him?

False witnesses did rise up; they laid to my charge things that I knew not.

They rewarded me evil for good to the spoiling of my soul.

But as for me, when they were sick, my clothing was sackcloth: I humbled my soul with fasting; and my prayer returned into mine own bosom.

I behaved myself as though he had been my friend or brother: I bowed down heavily, as one that mourneth for his mother.

But in mine adversity, they rejoiced, and gathered themselves together: yea, the abjects gathered themselves together against me, and I knew it not; they did tear me and ceased not: With hypocritical mockers in feasts, they gnashed upon me with their teeth.

Lord, how long wilt thou look on? rescue my soul from their destructions, my darling from the lions

I will give thee thanks in the great congregation: I will praise thee among much people.

Let not them that are mine enemies wrongfully rejoice over me: neither let them wink with the eye that hate me without a cause.

For they speak not peace: but they devise deceitful matters against them that are quiet in the land.

Yea, they opened their mouth wide against me, and said, Aha, aha, our eye hath seen it.

This thou hast seen, O LORD: keep not silence: O Lord, be not far from me.

Stir up thyself, and awake to my judgment, even unto my cause, my God and my Lord.

Judge me, O LORD my God, according to thy righteousness; and let them not rejoice over me.

Let them not say in their hearts, Ah, so would we have it: let them not say, we have swallowed him up.

Let them be ashamed and brought to confusion together that rejoice at mine hurt: let them be clothed with shame and dishonour that magnify themselves against me.

Let them shout for joy, and be glad, that favour my righteous cause: yea, let them say continually, Let the LORD be magnified, which hath pleasure in the prosperity of his servant.

And my tongue shall speak of thy righteousness and of thy praise all the day long."

Psalm 37:1-40 - Protection against enemies; against lies and slander (KJB)

"Fret not thyself because of evildoers, neither be thou envious against the workers of iniquity.

For they shall soon be cut down like the grass, and wither as the green herb.

Trust in the LORD, and do good; so shalt thou dwell in the land, and verily thou shalt be fed.

Delight thyself also in the LORD; and he shall give thee the desires of thine heart.

Commit thy way unto the LORD; trust also in him; and he shall bring it to pass.

And he shall bring forth thy righteousness as the light, and thy judgment as the noonday.

Rest in the LORD, and wait patiently for him: fret not thyself because of him who prospereth in his way, because of the man who bringeth wicked devices to pass.

Cease from anger, and forsake wrath: fret not thyself in any wise to do evil.

For evildoers shall be cut off: but those that wait upon the LORD, they shall inherit the earth.

For yet a little while, and the wicked shall not be: yea, thou shalt diligently consider his place, and it shall not be.

But the meek shall inherit the earth; and shall delight themselves in the abundance of peace.

The wicked plotteth against the just, and gnasheth upon him with his teeth.

The Lord shall laugh at him: for he seeth that his day is coming.

The wicked have drawn out the sword, and have bent their bow, to cast down the poor and needy, and to slay such as be of upright conversation.

Their sword shall enter into their own heart, and their bows shall be broken.

A little that a righteous man hath is better than the riches of many wicked.

For the arms of the wicked shall be broken: but the LORD upholdeth the righteous.

The LORD knoweth the days of the upright: and their inheritance shall be for ever.

They shall not be ashamed in the evil time: and in the days of famine they shall be satisfied.

But the wicked shall perish, and the enemies of the LORD shall be as the fat of lambs: they shall consume; into smoke shall they consume away.

The wicked borroweth, and payeth not again: but the righteous sheweth mercy, and giveth.

For such as be blessed of him shall inherit the earth; and they that be cursed of him shall be cut off.

The steps of a good man are ordered by the LORD: and he delighteth in his way.

Though he fall, he shall not be utterly cast down: for the LORD upholdeth him with his hand.

I have been young, and now am old; yet have I not seen the righteous forsaken, nor his seed begging bread.

He is ever merciful, and lendeth; and his seed is blessed.

Depart from evil, and do good; and dwell for evermore.

For the LORD loveth judgment, and forsaketh not his saints; they are preserved for ever: but the seed of the wicked shall be cut off.

The righteous shall inherit the land, and dwell therein forever.

The mouth of the righteous speaketh wisdom, and his tongue talketh of judgment.

The law of his God is in his heart; none of his steps shall slide.

The wicked watcheth the righteous, and seeketh to slay him.

The LORD will not leave him in his hand, nor condemn him when he is judged.

Wait on the LORD, and keep his way, and he shall exalt thee to inherit the land: when the wicked are cut off, thou shalt see it.

I have seen the wicked in great power, and spreading himself like a green bay tree.

Yet he passed away, and, lo, he was not: yea, I sought him, but he could not be found.

Mark the perfect man, and behold the upright: for the end of that man is peace.

But the transgressors shall be destroyed together: the end of the wicked shall be cut off.

But the salvation of the righteous is of the LORD: he is their strength in the time of trouble.

And the LORD shall help them and deliver them: he shall deliver them from the wicked, and save them, because they trust in him."

Psalm 59:1-17 – For protection against falsehoods and enemies (KJB)

"Deliver me from mine enemies, O my God: defend me from them that rise up against me.

Deliver me from the workers of iniquity and save me from bloody men.

For, lo, they lie in wait for my soul: the mighty are gathered against me; not for my transgression, nor for my sin, O LORD.

They run and prepare themselves without my fault: awake to help me and behold.

Thou therefore, O LORD God of hosts, the God of Israel, awake to visit all the heathen: be not merciful to any wicked transgressors. Selah.

They return at evening: they make a noise like a dog and go round about the city.

Behold, they belch out with their mouth: swords are in their lips: for who, say they, doth hear?

But thou, O LORD, shalt laugh at them; thou shalt have all the heathen in derision.

Because of his strength will I wait upon thee: for God is my defense.

The God of my mercy shall prevent me: God shall let me see my desire upon mine enemies.

Slay them not, lest my people forget: scatter them by thy power; and bring them down, O Lord our shield.

For the sin of their mouth and the words of their lips let them even be taken in their pride: and for cursing and lying which, they speak.

Consume them in wrath, consume them, that they may not be: and let them know that God ruleth in Jacob unto the ends of the earth. Selah.

And at evening let them return; and let them make a noise like a dog and go round about the city.

Let them wander up and down for meat, and grudge if they be not satisfied.

But I will sing of thy power; yea, I will sing aloud of thy mercy in the morning: for thou hast been my defense and refuge in the day of my trouble.

Unto thee, O my strength, will I sing: for God is my defense, and the God of my mercy."

Psalm 64: 1- 10 Protection from enemies (KJB)

"Hear my voice, O God, in my prayer: preserve my life from fear of the enemy.

Hide me from the secret counsel of the wicked; from the insurrection of the workers of iniquity:

Who whet their tongue like a sword, and bend their bows to shoot their arrows, even bitter words:

That they may shoot in secret at the perfect: suddenly do they shoot at him, and fear not.

They encourage themselves in an evil matter: they commune of laying snares privily; they say, who shall see them?

They search out iniquities; they accomplish a diligent search: both the inward thought of every one of them, and the heart, is deep.

But God shall shoot at them with an arrow; suddenly shall they be wounded.

So, they shall make their own tongue to fall upon themselves: all that see them shall flee away.

And all men shall fear and shall declare the work of God; for they shall wisely consider of his doing.

The righteous shall be glad in the Lord and shall trust in him; and all the upright in heart shall glory."

Psalm 65:1-13 - For fortune and success in gambling (KJB)

"Praise waiteth for thee, O God, in Sion: and unto thee shall the vow be performed.

O thou that hearest prayer, unto thee shall all flesh come.

Iniquities prevail against me: as for our transgressions, thou shalt purge them away.

Blessed is the man whom thou choosest, and causest to approach unto thee, that he may dwell
in thy courts: we shall be satisfied with the goodness of thy house, even of thy holy temple.

By terrible things in righteousness wilt thou answer us, O God of our salvation; who art the
confidence of all the ends of the earth, and of them that are afar off upon the sea:
Which by his strength setteth fast the mountains; being girded with power:
Which stilleth the noise of the seas, the noise of their waves, and the tumult of the people.

They also that dwell in the uttermost parts are afraid at thy tokens: thou makest the outgoings of
the morning and evening to rejoice.

Thou visitest the earth, and waterest it: thou greatly enrichest it with the river of God, which is
full of water: thou preparest them corn, when thou hast so provided for it.

Thou waterest the ridges thereof abundantly: thou settlest the furrows thereof: thou makest it
soft with showers: thou blessest the springing thereof.

Thou crownest the year with thy goodness; and thy paths drop fatness.

They drop upon the pastures of the wilderness: and the little hills rejoice on every side.

The pastures are clothed with flocks; the valleys also are covered over with corn; they shout for
joy, they also sing."

Psalm 69: 1-36 - To overcome addictions and make whole (KJB)

Save me, O God; for the waters are come in unto my soul.

I sink in deep mire, where there is no standing: I am come into deep waters, where the floods
overflow me.

I am weary of my crying: my throat is dried: mine eyes fail while I wait for my God.

They that hate me without a cause are more than the hairs of mine head: they that would destroy
me, being mine enemies wrongfully, are mighty: then I restored that which I took not away.

O God, thou knowest my foolishness; and my sins are not hid from thee.

Let not them that wait on thee, O Lord GOD of hosts, be ashamed for my sake: let not those that seek thee be confounded for my sake, O God of Israel.

Because for thy sake I have borne reproach; shame hath covered my face.

I am become a stranger unto my brethren, and an alien unto my mother's children.

For the zeal of thine house hath eaten me up; and the reproaches of them that reproached thee are fallen upon me.

When I wept, and chastened my soul with fasting, that was to my reproach.

I made sackcloth also my garment; and I became a proverb to them.

They that sit in the gate speak against me; and I was the song of the drunkards.

But as for me, my prayer is unto thee, O LORD, in an acceptable time: O God, in the multitude of thy mercy hear me, in the truth of thy salvation.

Deliver me out of the mire, and let me not sink: let me be delivered from them that hate me, and out of the deep waters.

Let not the waterflood overflow me, neither let the deep swallow me up, and let not the pit shut her mouth upon me.

Hear me, O LORD; for thy lovingkindness is good: turn unto me according to the multitude of thy tender mercies.

And hide not thy face from thy servant; for I am in trouble: hear me speedily.

Draw nigh unto my soul, and redeem it: deliver me because of mine enemies.

Thou hast known my reproach, and my shame, and my dishonour: mine adversaries are all before thee.

Reproach hath broken my heart; and I am full of heaviness: and I looked for some to take pity, but there was none; and for comforters, but I found none.

They gave me also gall for my meat; and in my thirst they gave me vinegar to drink.

Let their table become a snare before them: and that which should have been for their welfare, let it become a trap.

Let their eyes be darkened, that they see not; and make their loins continually to shake.

Pour out thine indignation upon them, and let thy wrathful anger take hold of them.

Let their habitation be desolate; and let none dwell in their tents.

For they persecute him whom thou hast smitten; and they talk to the grief of those whom thou hast wounded.

Add iniquity unto their iniquity: and let them not come into thy righteousness.

Let them be blotted out of the book of the living, and not be written with the righteous.

But I am poor and sorrowful: let thy salvation, O God, set me up on high.

I will praise the name of God with a song, and will magnify him with thanksgiving.

This also shall please the LORD better than an ox or bullock that hath horns and hoofs.

The humble shall see this, and be glad: and your heart shall live that seek God.

For the LORD heareth the poor, and despiseth not his prisoners.

Let the heaven and earth praise him, the seas, and everything that moveth therein.

For God will save Zion, and will build the cities of Judah: that they may dwell there, and have it in possession.

The seed also of his servants shall inherit it: and they that love his name shall dwell therein."

Psalms 70: 1-5 - Protection from enemies (KJB)

"Make haste, O God, to deliver me; make haste to help me, O LORD.

Let them be ashamed and confounded that seek after my soul: let them be turned backward, and put to confusion, that desire my hurt.

Let them be turned back for a reward of their shame that say, Aha, aha.

Let all those that seek thee rejoice and be glad in thee: and let such as love thy salvation say continually, Let God be magnified

But I am poor and needy: make haste unto me, O God: thou art my help and my deliverer; O LORD, make no tarrying."

Psalms 94:1-23 – To repel evil (KJB)

"O LORD God, to whom vengeance belongeth; O God, to whom vengeance belongeth, shew thyself.

Lift up thyself, thou judge of the earth: render a reward to the proud.

LORD, how long shall the wicked, how long shall the wicked triumph?

How long shall they utter and speak hard things? and all the workers of iniquity boast themselves?

They break in pieces thy people, O LORD, and afflict thine heritage.

They slay the widow and the stranger, and murder the fatherless.

Yet they say, The LORD shall not see, neither shall the God of Jacob regard it.

Understand, ye brutish among the people: and ye fools, when will ye be wise?

He that planted the ear, shall he not hear? he that formed the eye, shall he not see?

He that chastiseth the heathen, shall not he correct? he that teacheth man knowledge, shall not he know?

The LORD knoweth the thoughts of man, that they are vanity.

Blessed is the man whom thou chastenest, O LORD, and teachest him out of thy law;
That thou mayest give him rest from the days of adversity, until the pit be digged for the wicked.

For the LORD will not cast off his people, neither will he forsake his inheritance.

But judgment shall return unto righteousness: and all the upright in heart shall follow it.

Who will rise up for me against the evildoers? or who will stand up for me against the workers of iniquity?

Unless the LORD had been my help, my soul had almost dwelt in silence.

When I said, My foot slippeth; thy mercy, O LORD, held me up.

In the multitude of my thoughts within me thy comforts delight my soul.

Shall the throne of iniquity have fellowship with thee, which frameth mischief by a law?

They gather themselves together against the soul of the righteous, and condemn the innocent blood.

But the LORD is my defence; and my God is the rock of my refuge.

And he shall bring upon them their own iniquity, and shall cut them off in their own wickedness; yea, the LORD our God shall cut them off."

Psalms 126:1-6 - To promote fertility (KJB)

"When the LORD turned again the captivity of Zion, we were like them that dream.

Then was our mouth filled with laughter, and our tongue with singing: then said they among the heathen, The LORD hath done great things for them.

The LORD hath done great things for us; whereof we are glad.

Turn again our captivity, O LORD, as the streams in the south.

They that sow in tears shall reap in joy.

He that goeth forth and weepeth, bearing precious seed, shall doubtless come again with rejoicing, bringing his sheaves with him."

Psalms 127:1-5 - For protection of children; fertility (KJB)

"Except the LORD build the house, they labour in vain that build it: except the LORD keep the city, the watchman waketh but in vain.

It is vain for you to rise up early, to sit up late, to eat the bread of sorrows: for so he giveth his beloved sleep.

Lo, children are an heritage of the LORD: and the fruit of the womb is his reward.

As arrows are in the hand of a mighty man; so are children of the youth.

Happy is the man that hath his quiver full of them: they shall not be ashamed, but they shall speak with the enemies in the gate."

Psalm 139:1-24 - For protection (KJB)

"O Lord, thou hast searched me, and known me.

Thou knowest my downsitting and mine uprising, thou understandest my thought afar off.

Thou compassest my path and my lying down, and art acquainted with all my ways.

For there is not a word in my tongue, but, lo, O Lord, thou knowest it altogether.

Thou hast beset me behind and before and laid thine hand upon me.

Such knowledge is too wonderful for me; it is high, I cannot attain unto it.

Whither shall I go from thy spirit? or whither shall I flee from thy presence?

If I ascend up into heaven, thou art there: if I make my bed in hell, behold, thou art there.

If I take the wings of the morning, and dwell in the uttermost parts of the sea;

Even there shall thy hand lead me, and thy right hand shall hold me.

If I say, Surely the darkness shall cover me; even the night shall be light about me.

Yea, the darkness hideth not from thee; but the night shineth as the day: the darkness and the light are both alike to thee.

For thou hast possessed my reins: thou hast covered me in my mother's womb.

I will praise thee; for I am fearfully and wonderfully made: marvellous are thy works; and that my soul knoweth right well.

My substance was not hid from thee, when I was made in secret, and curiously wrought in the lowest parts of the earth.

Thine eyes did see my substance yet being unperfect; and in thy book all my members were written, which in continuance were fashioned, when as yet there was none of them.

How precious also are thy thoughts unto me, O God! how great is the sum of them!

If I should count them, they are more in number than the sand: when I awake, I am still with thee.

Surely, thou wilt slay the wicked, O God: depart from me therefore, ye bloody men.

For they speak against thee wickedly, and thine enemies take thy name in vain.

Do not I hate them, O Lord, that hate thee? and am not I grieved with those that rise up against thee?

I hate them with perfect hatred: I count them mine enemies.

Search me, O God, and know my heart: try me, and know my thoughts:

And see if there be any wicked way in me and lead me in the way everlasting."

Psalms 144: 1-15 - For healing and protection in conflict (KJB)

"Blessed be the LORD my strength, which teacheth my hands to war, and my fingers to fight:

My goodness, and my fortress; my high tower, and my deliverer; my shield, and he in whom I trust; who subdueth my people under me.

LORD, what is man, that thou takest knowledge of him! or the son of man, that thou makest account of him!

Man is like to vanity: his days are as a shadow that passeth away.

Bow thy heavens, O LORD, and come down: touch the mountains, and they shall smoke.

Cast forth lightning, and scatter them: shoot out thine arrows, and destroy them.

Send thine hand from above; rid me, and deliver me out of great waters, from the hand of strange children; Whose mouth speaketh vanity, and their right hand is a right hand of falsehood.

I will sing a new song unto thee, O God: upon a psaltery and an instrument of ten strings will I sing praises unto thee.

It is he that giveth salvation unto kings: who delivereth David his servant from the hurtful sword.

Rid me, and deliver me from the hand of strange children, whose mouth speaketh vanity, and their right hand is a right hand of falsehood:

That our sons may be as plants grown up in their youth; that our daughters may be as corner stones, polished after the similitude of a palace:

That our garners may be full, affording all manner of store: that our sheep may bring forth thousands and ten thousands in our streets:

That our oxen may be strong to labour; that there be no breaking in, nor going out; that there be no complaining in our streets.

Happy is that people, that is in such a case: yea, happy is that people, whose God is the LORD."

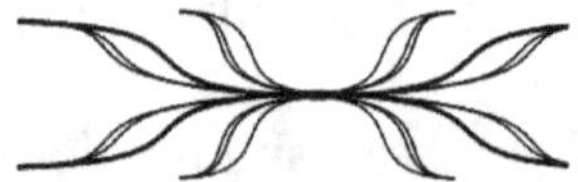

US National Archives and Records Administration

Carolina Dye – Known as Aunt Caroline
1810 - 1918.
Hoodoo practitioner,
Seer and Spiritualist

Some Hoodoo

Referred to by many as conjure, rootwork or witchcraft, Hoodoo is used for the building of personal spiritual power and to create a balance in which neither good nor evil can dominate. They venerate their own ancestors as well as animal spirits on their altars. Archangels are called upon during root workings. Meeting Death is known as "walking the path of bones." Their god has no gender or any concern for the troubles of mankind. Lesser spirits are invoked to help resolve the problems of men. The bible is known as the great conjure book where Moses is the great conjurer or Hoodoo man. *The Secrets of Psalms* is also an important written work as it teaches people to communicate with god and his minions through prayer. This traditional folk magic blends African traditions, Native American beliefs and the Christian bible.

Workings using the Bible

*Reciting Psalm 3 in a spiritual prayer is used to banish troublesome and oppressive spirits. It is also said over healing teas. A prayer sometimes follows:

"May the Lord be my physician and helper. In the name of all that is merciful, heal me from the pain that runs through my body and give me peace. Amen. " +++

*Psalm 4 is recited three times before sunrise for luck and seven times for business gains. While reciting Psalm 4, print a wish on a piece of brown paper bag and burn it in a bowl. Take the ashes outside and scatter them. The wind will take your request.

"May the lord allow me to prosper and my wishes to be satisfied? Amen." +++

*Three days before your case is brought before the judge, light a small blue or brown candle and recite Psalm 5. These can also be anointed with High John oil. It must be done before each sunrise and at each sunset in order to have a successful outcome.

A prayer can be added: "May the Lord grant me with protection, so the judge may regard me with grace. Amen."

*Use Psalm 6 verse 2 to heal a broken bone. Say this prayer each day.

"Have mercy upon me, O Lord, for I am weak: O Lord, heal me, for my bones are vexed."

Added request and prayer**: "Lord, hear my prayer. Mend my bones and heal my body in your name. Amen."**

*Psalm 7 Verses 1through 10 is used to break a hex. Use black or purple candles for hex breaking. Get a cup of well or spring water. As you recite the psalm, pour the water out in the direction of where you think it came from.

Extra prayer: "Deliver me O Lord, cast away this evil brought upon me and grant me peace. Amen. +++

*Psalm 11 and Psalm 12 are used in prayer for protection from persecution.

*Psalm 23 is recited for money drawing. A small green candle is anointed with bayberry oil and lit each day. The prayer must be said for seven mornings in a row as soon as you wake up.

Extra prayer: "God grant me abundance and peace. May the Lord protect me from ill winds and clear the way for me to see true. Amen."

*Psalms 29, 23, and 91, are used to get rid of a troublesome spirit. Read these psalms and order the offending spirit to depart. Finish with a prayer:

"Quiet this restless spirit, O Lord. Hear my prayer as thou once did that of thy servants, Moses and David, and restore peace to ___ child of ___ for the sake of thy holy name El-Shaddai. Amen. +++

*Use Psalm 29 verse 3 and 4 for protection from oncoming thunder and storms.

"The voice of the LORD is upon the waters, the God of glory thundereth, the LORD is upon many waters. The voice of the LORD is powerful; the voice of the LORD is full of majesty."

*All of Psalm 30 for protection from evil.

* Use Psalm 119 verses 17 through 24 to attract luck. It is said seven times to attract luck for gambling.

Deal bountifully with thy servant, that I may live, and keep thy word.

Open thou mine eyes, that I may behold wondrous things out of thy law.

I am a stranger in the earth: hide not thy commandments from me.

My soul breaketh for the longing that it hath unto thy judgments at all times.

Thou hast rebuked the proud that are cursed, which do err from thy commandments.

Remove from me reproach and contempt; for I have kept thy testimonies.

Princes also did sit and speak against me: but thy servant did meditate in thy statutes.

Thy testimonies also are my delight and my counselors.

Use of Candles in Hoodoo

If you are using oil on a candle, take a couple of drops and rub them in between your palms. Grasping the candle, start at the middle and work the oil downward. Then return to the middle and work upward to the top. If you are trying to break a spell or curse, reverse the oiling process. Work towards the top first and then the lower part of the candle. Candles in glass containers are treated differently. Wash the outside of the glass with alcohol. Then, take a drop of oil and rub it on the top of the candle clockwise, thinking about your intent. Do not forget to look at the moon's phase when doing a working. Waxing moon attracts, and waning moon repels. You can also put dried herbs or stone powder on top of your candles.

The Flame Talks

In Hoodoo or pagan rituals, it is told that you need to pay attention to the way a candle is burning or "talking." This insures that your working is creating the right results.

If the flame is strong – Energy, power and success in your working. It is also positive if the flame is high and stable; outside energies could be helping you.

If the flame is weak – Energy is being pulled away. You may have to make sacrifices to get what you want. There may be someone opposing you.

If the flame jumps and dances – Outside influences are trying to take control. You may have to confront problems you were not expecting in this working. Results may not be what you wish.

If your candle makes noise during your working – The spirits you wish to contact are trying to communicate with you.

If the flame puffs or creates white smoke – Someone is working against you. Be on guard.

A flame that is blue - The presence of protective spirits.

A flame that fades in and out – A ghost or spirit wanting to make its presence known.

A broken flame – This can occur when the wick breaks off while burning or if the fiber splits in the wick and you end up with two flames. Someone close to you will leave you or may pass away.

A flame that suddenly goes out – If there is no draft and this occurs, stop your working. It will be unsuccessful.

Candle Trivia and Spirituality

- White, blue, purple, rose or red candles are used by Christians on the Christmas Advent wreath. One was burned each week of the four weeks before Christmas. The fifth candle burned on Christmas eve is white and represents (purity) Christ.
- White candles are burned as a votive offering or prayer requests for God's intervention in the Catholic faith.
- In older German and Scandinavian traditions, candles lit in the darkness of winter were a hope of the returning spring.
- Used in both Christian as well as pagan beliefs, candles of saints have been used for prayer, direction or intent.

Colored Candles for Spell-Work:

- Silver candles are used for communication with ancestors.

- White candles are used for clearing negativity.

- Red, pink and white candles are usually used for marriage.

- Brown candles are used for finding lost objects.

- Red candles are burned in a spell for strength against enemies.

- Brown candles are burnt for animal healings.

- White and light blue candles are for sending calmness and peace.

- Gray candles are used for dreamwork and visions.

- Orange candles are used for job hunting spells.

- White, red and black candles are used during Samhain to represent the maiden, mother and the old woman or crone.

- Red and Black candles are burned for reversing a spell.

- Use yellow candles are used for overcoming addiction spells.

- Indigo candles are used for stopping gossip, lies and jealousy.

- Orange candles are used for justice, court cases and investments.

- Burn pink candles for self love.

- Black candles are used for hexing or clearing away things

- Green, yellow brown or silver candles are used in gambling

- Orange, yellow and green together is used to strenghten creative money-making energy.

- Green candles are for money or growth.

- Pink and light blue candles traditionally represent "girl" or "boy."

- Yellow, purple and blue candles are used for astral travel.

Serpents and Prayer

In Appalachian rural areas, some churches still prepare for a ceremony of great faith as well as extreme danger. Many Holiness, Pentecostals and Evangelicals (including Charismatics) believe that if the Holy Spirit was within a person, they should be able to "take up" (handle) rattlesnakes or other venomous serpents without fear. Though it is only a small part of the religious service, the practice of snake handling convinced the congregation of evidence of an individual's salvation and faith in God. Their proof that they should take part in this ritual comes from two passages from the Old Testament and one passage in the New Testament:

"And these signs shall follow them that believe: In my name shall they cast out devils; they shall speak with new tongues. They shall take up serpents; and if they drink any deadly thing, it shall not hurt them; they shall lay hands on the sick, and they shall recover." **Book of Mark 16:17 through 18**

"Behold, I give unto you power to tread on serpents and scorpions, and over all the power of the enemy: and nothing shall by any means hurt you." **Book of Luke 10:19**

In Acts 28:1-6, Paul was bitten by a poisonous snake and came to no harm:

"And when Paul had gathered a bundle of sticks, and laid them on the fire, there came a viper out of the heat, and fastened on his hand. And when the barbarians saw the venomous beast hang on his hand, they said among themselves, No doubt this man is a murderer, whom, though he hath escaped the sea, yet vengeance suffereth not to live. And he shook off the beast into the fire, and felt no harm. Howbeit they looked when he should have swollen, or fallen down dead suddenly: but after they had looked a great while, and saw no harm come to him, they changed their minds, and said that he was a god."

Singing, dancing and praying during the ceremony brings about the ability to speak in tongues, the testimony of miracles and laying on hands for healing. This happens when a congregant is "touched" by the Holy Spirit.

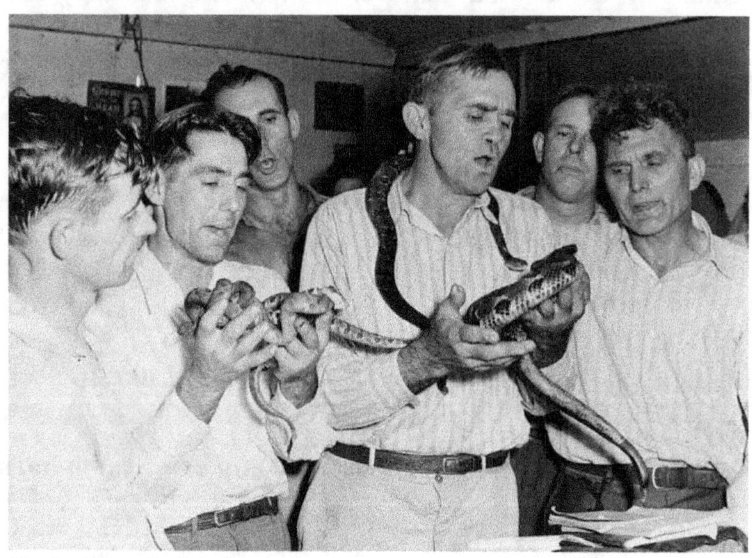

Kentucky snake handlers
1946 - Courtesy of U.S. National Archives

Appalachian Midwives and Folk Healing Ways

This unique use of the four elements, prayer and spell work, along with practical knowledge, is common in mountain "Doctoring or Granny" healing. Known for being self or community-taught, these midwives or "Grannies" of the mountain regions created their own legends for their unselfish acts of community survival.

Molly Buck's story

"Daddy said that when I was born, the Granny laid me in between my mother's legs while she rinsed out the rag she was washing me with. Smiling, she had just announced I was born with a caul on my face. As soon as my daddy bent over to see, I let out a squeal, flung my hands up and ripped that caul clear off! Laughing, the Granny proclaimed I was to be a powerful one."

Taking a sip of coffee, Molly Buck continued, "When Pa told me this story, I was ten years old and had already been working with my mother and father for two years. I had gotten pretty good with it..." Good memories.

Jamie looked up from his notebook and grinned. Molly thought he was such an intense fella for one so young but I guess that is why he is sitting at my kitchen right now, writing it down. Jamie Bradshaw is the young journalist who has appeared in some of my stories. He came to interview me on Granny magic and birthing three years ago, and young man was still coming around. He wants to learn the cunning ways and seems to have a knack for it.

He and David, my grandson, can roam the hills all day and bring me back their "treasures" like two little kids, rather than young men they are. They're a wonder. Jamie sat quietly across the table from me writing down Daddy's story. Looking out her window as she sat in her old cushioned chair, the elderly woman quietly said, "The Lord has made my life complete."

Her eyes had been a witness of many a-change. Big cities were growing up everywhere, machines and families scattering. Many good things still left, but there is question in the new. God's light still shines and my work in the community has not ceased. The old ways are still good. Our daughters and granddaughters come to take our place when we die. Faith in God and in the old ways still stands together.

She looked up as the young man repeated his question. "Pardon? Where was I born? Born in Silva, North Carolina on October 7, 1939. My mother was staying with her sister while my Daddy was helping a neighbor back here with the harvesting of sweet corn and melons. My mam sure ate a lot of melons before I was born. Cantaloupe was her favorite. Mine, too. She died of TB in 1951. Daddy wasn't so happy after that. Sometimes I would catch him staring out into space all quiet-like. My father died five years later after I had married my husband Owen. I don't think he wanted to stay. That's what the Healer Man had told us. He said Pa just wanted to be with my Mam.

My daughter Louise was born the next year and though my husband was a good family provider and worked the land, he started working in the mines as well, a couple of days a week. I still remember the day he died; one of the tunnels had caved partially in. Owen volunteered to go down into the hole and help the others clean the passage, so they could get back to work. Not ten minutes later, the whole end of that tunnel collapsed. There were eighteen of them. All young; all dead.

It took a while but once the grief was over, Molly realized that she was a twenty-three year old mother without a husband, living in an area where she had better learn to work even harder to make a living for her child. For years, she wove cloth for the community and dipped candles for the market to sell. She had started working with the Grannies when she was fifteen being a "fetch and carry." The ways of childbirth had now become common place for her. Now, she needed to talk to Granny Erinde.

Granny Erinde was in her early sixties and was one of the oldest Granny women still birthing. Molly went to her cabin with a jar of plum butter she had canned and a pan of biscuits. Granny Erinde was in her garden when Molly approached. She had a half of basket of tomatoes in her arms when she walked up to the girl.

"How are you doin', Molly?"

"Doin' the best with what God gave me and you?"

"I'm blessed. Come inside, Molly, and have a glass of tea."

"Yes Mam, thank you."

Going inside, Molly sat down at the table while the older woman poured the tea over the ice in the glasses. Handing her one, she sat down on the other side of the table. Molly laid the plum butter and the biscuits out in front of them. Granny Erinde said, "The Lord be praised!" as she took the gifts. Laying some paper bags on the table, she put a biscuit on each one of them and got a spoon for the plum butter. After a short prayer, the women ate until there wasn't a crumb left. Then, setting back in her chair, the older healer and mid-wife waited for me to start the discussion.

I looked up at her and said, "I want to learn from you. My Mam's mother was a Granny. I want to be one too."

"Are you sure about this? She said. You will be giving up a lot. You won't have much time to socialize and how do you know you won't want another husband? You just lost yours." The tears welled up in my eyes.

Taking a sip of tea, she continued, "Molly, I've seen you working with the other Grannies, easing women in the birth bed. You've got the power of the Holy Spirit in you. I heered your grandma did too."

She walked over to my side of the table and put her hand under my chin, turned my face up, and looked into my watery eyes.

"Well, you definitely understand grief. You wouldn't be drawn to this work if you didn't. Are you sure you want to do this, Molly? You might be able to get a job in town. You have a lot of family around..."

"Yes, Mam, I want to do this. Will you let me work with you?"

"Are you willing to work with me for, say, three years?" I nodded.

"Then, come to me when you are on the first day of your next moon (lunar cycle). The lessons will begin then. Sun up. At my house. Dress for digging just in case."

Two Mondays later, I returned to her door. She greeted me as I entered the room. Then Granny Erinde took both my hands, bowed her head and recited a piece of scripture. It was from the book of Matthew in the bible.

She said, **"Truly I say to you, whatever you bind on earth shall have been bound in heaven; and whatever you loose on earth shall have been loosed in heaven."**
"Amen." I said. She looked up and let go of my hands.

As we sat at her table, she began. "There was a time that a woman in these hills died early and alone in the birthing bed. Those that birthed themselves usually had little chance of their child livin'. We have been fortunate that many of the birthing ways that we were taught as Grannies came from the Native American peoples that were already here, as well as our Scotch-Irish and Welsh ancestors that settled in these hills. We have learned from the good earth many of the things that help us survive here as well.

We were taught by involving ourselves with many of the families that surround us in the community. Our ways are Christian, but our ways are also the old ways. With the use of folk medicine, cleanliness and prayer, most of our children around here live. The women who take on the responsibility of being a Granny must endure a lot of things: hard work, a lack of sleep, and through all the children you have birthed and all families you helped grow strong become your family too, there will be little time for one of your own. Death will stand next to you each time you help a child take their first breath. You will mourn those who pass and help their souls on their way. You will create medicines and charms to keep the community safe. You will know much and you will teach much. Nature is your partner in healing. You have been taught the cunning ways from your mother and conjure from your father. Your medicines heal. You have the power of God within you. Do you still want to do this?"

"Yes, I do."

And that was the beginning and I've never looked back. I worked hard and became a needed member of the community. Many consult me and I am blessed. I am a Granny. Now called Granny Buck by most. Even now, I look back and I can see myself as a young woman again, just coming home from foraging or birthing a new member of the community. I worked hard to be a healer and my family turned out real good. My big sister Jeanne would smile and my little daughter would greet me at the door and with shouts of, "Ma! Ma!" I again see in my mind, my daughter's small body as she flies towards my open arms.

****

I think I dozed off. Jamie is gently shaking me. As I look up, he reaches over and turns off the video equipment. I get up from the chair and pull my sweater closer to me.

"Sun's almost down. It's neared time for bed. Can you come by tomorrow to finish this?"

The young man grinned, "Sure, Granny. Whatever you want. Is David going to drop by tomorrow?"

"About four. Come by and I'll fix somethin'."

"You bet." Collecting up his things, he headed for the door.

Molly walked towards the door with him. "Drive slow on those back roads, Jamie. The does are in heat and you don't want an accident with a deer."

As he drove away, she went back inside, tamped the fire, and went to bed.

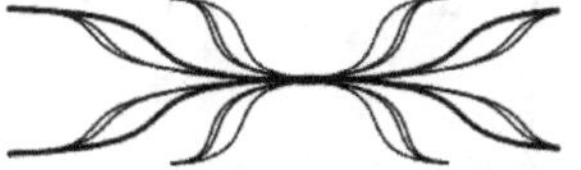

Healing, Preventive and Magical Trivia

* Finding a "holey" stone on the ground is good luck. This is a natural stone with a hole worn through it. Those who wear one around their neck believe they can be cured of many diseases. It is also used to keep fairies away. Many hang a holey stone over the crib to protect their babies.

* Drops of urine in an infected ear are used to get rid of the infection.

* Corn silk tea was used by Grannies to ease a woman in childbirth. It induces contractions of the uterus.

* Drink mare's milk to cure Whooping Cough.

* Some Grannies were known to give a newborn a pinch of ash. This should be done while the child is breastfeeding. It is said to give lifelong protection against witchcraft.

* Swabbing a baby's mouth out with its own wet diaper can get rid of thrush. It's said a twin can blow in a baby's mouth and get rid of it, too. Blackberry tea in the baby's bottle is used as well.

* To fade out age spots or freckles, find and collect some fresh Honeysuckle leaves and flowers. A good handful soaked in water overnight makes a great face rinse and fades out the spots.

*A toasted piece of bread is moistened with vinegar and is then placed on the chest to cure Bronchitis.

* Put a half of a raw onion in a sick room. It will kill bacteria.

* Snakeskin is wrapped around the thigh of a pregnant woman to quicken labor.

* A sweet gum twig dipped in whiskey is good for cleaning teeth.

* Granny women were known to prescribe powdered eggshell to be taken internally to ease PMS symptoms.

* Nine pinches of dried mountain moss, powdered up, is mixed with nine pinches of ashes from the hearth. Mixed with whey and eaten, it is said to cure inflammation.

* Drink parsley water to get rid of kidney stones.

* Place a wet teabag on a sting. Leave tea bag on until the swelling from the sting goes down. The stinger will then be easy to remove.

* **T**o keep ants away from weak or start-up bee colonies, lay mint, catnip or pennyroyal on top of the inner cover of the bee box. Another herb used is wormwood. Wormwood eliminates the human odor from a beekeeper's hands allowing easier access to the hive.

* **S**tepping over a newborn could stunt their growth.

* **B**oil Peach leaves and drink as a tea for ten days. It will help heal up your eczema.

* **G**round up peach kernels and vinegar are mixed together and placed on a person's scalp to regrow hair.

* **S**ilk from the purple thistle is used during emergencies to staunch the flow of blood. The silk can be collected in autumn from the thistle's dried flowers.

* **D**rinking water distilled from peach flowers gets rid of worms in the body.

* **I**f you need to get rid of a sty on your eye, rub garlic on it

* **E**at a mixture of mashed chestnuts and sugar to ease your rheumatism.

* **S**ome mothers were known to spit on their newborn babies to bring good luck.

* **A** newborn's hair was not cut during the first few weeks of its life for fear it would die.

* **M**int repels rodents and can be used as an ant barrier.

* **R**ub watermelon rind on a poison ivy rash to get rid of it. Banana peel works well, too.

* **P**regnant women should never look at a deceased person or it will mark the unborn child.

Miscellaneous

* **B**urn cedar and pine logs in the fireplace to attract prosperity.

* **P**aint your door or front porch ceiling "haint" blue (a light sky blue or some say Carolina blue) to discourage evil at your door. The color is also used to trick wasps and spiders from nesting on ceilings. This originated through African-Gullah folk traditions and can be found through the southeastern mountain areas as well as southern coasts.

* **I**f you find a dead owl, it means that you recently escaped a bad illness or even possibly death.

* **W**hen framing the door of your cabin, use elm wood. It is used to repel evil.

* **P**utting pots of fern on your porch keeps curses away.

* **H**eaven's Letter is a strong form of Hoodoo protection. It is a magical chain-letter filled with charms and bible quotes.

* **L**ittle John root is also known as Little John to Chew. It is said that the galangal root sweetens the breath and eases the stomach, but it is most famous for the use of winning court cases. Spit some saliva after chewing the root onto the courthouse floor, and you're sure to win your case. I would advise that you do this before the judge enters the room.

* **I**f you see thorns in a dream, it may be warning you of bad luck.

* **T**o turn away thieves, place a saucer above the front door.

* **B**urn oak wood in the fireplace to protect the home against natural disasters.

* **T**o break a blockage:

  Joshua 6:20- "So the people shouted when the priests blew with the trumpets: and it came to pass, when the people heard the sound of the trumpet, and the people shouted with a great shout, that the wall fell down flat, so that the people went up into the city, every man straight before him, and they took the city." This should be read for seven days. (On the first day read seven time, next day six... all the way to seventh day and after that reading say:" **By faith the walls of Jericho fell, after the people had marched around them for seven days."**

  Hebrews 11: 30

* **A** seventh son can heal and talk to spirits.

* **M**any mountain folks believed that a dead person's soul remained with their body for 24 hours after they die. Family and friends watched over the body the first day after death to make sure the devil did not steal the deceased's soul before it could leave.

* **H**oodoo is a mixture of African and Native American folk magic.

Crossroads, Graveyards and a Bone n' Bits Bag

I guess it speaks for itself...

I'll meet you at the Crossroads...

Late in the evenings of September or October, you may notice several dug-up areas beside Appalachian or Smoky mountain roads where two or more of these roads meet and cross over each other. If it were possible for you to look underneath the turned soil, you may find boxes or cloth pouches filled with things such as herbs or roots, photographs, animal bones, stones or dirt; each box or packet petitioning whatever spirit, god or devil they can invoke with their requests. At the darkest part of night (12:00 midnight), many say, they have seen a flash of a shadow; the hair on their necks standing up as they realize that they may be in the presence of a wandering spirit, "The Black Man", "Old Nick", or even the goddess Hecate.

The Black Man is an African trickster spirit introduced into mountain folklore through runaway slaves and freemen that settled or worked in the area. To meet him with a request, you must bring something associated with what you want; perhaps a picture of someone you love or desire, or a deed if you want property. Go alone at night for nine executive nights and observe. Be warned, for the Black Man is a shape shifter/shadow figure and is known to appear as a black dog with great red eyes or some other type of dark animal in the night. If he does not scare you off by the ninth night, he is supposed to appear in human form and then you will be able to speak to him of your request. If it is granted, the request will not come without a price: usually it is seven years of service to the Black Man.

The crossroads are considered to be a powerful spot where the realm of the spirit world and the world of man meets. It is believed that dark entities will appear to those who go there, hoping to make a deal. Many who practice magic, know it is sometimes required to go to a crossroads to work on a spell or a root. Some people just collect soil from a crossroads for themselves or others to use.

The idea of a "Devil" or "Old Nick" being called to the crossroads comes from Christian belief. He represents the dark or negative force of Christianity's spiritual nature. Stories are told that he would make appearances at a crossroads when called, in order make a deal with anyone in exchange for their immortal soul. Probably the most famous folk story of all pertaining to the Devil and his deals, is about guitar player Robert Johnson (1911-1938). Johnson, famous for his delta blues guitar playing, was thought to have met the Devil at a crossroad and sold his soul to become a great musician. Crossroads are considered places of power and have been for thousands of years.

The idea that dark goddesses haunted the crossroads goes far back into history. Roman mythology had the goddess Trivia, who would appear at cemeteries and crossroads. She was the dark goddess of witchcraft and wandered about in the night; noticed only by dogs who would howl or by wild animals who would act with alarm.

Another well-known goddess is Hecate. She is also known as "the Crone" or "Dark Lady" in many American pagan beliefs. This Greek goddess is said to appear at crossroads where three or more roads cross over each other. Most people will petition her in a dark, wooded, secluded area during the Harvest moon. She is associated with sorcery and death.

Thanks to Simy27

As to places of power, Native American Indian mounds and stone circles still exist through the Appalachian mountain range and hikers have been known to lose time while hiking by or residing around them. It is said they act as magical portals.

Moundsville, West Virginia.

Graveyards

Courtesy of U.S. National Archives

Listen for things that are not spoken and watch for things not there...

Graveyards and cemeteries have always been strong places of spiritual essence. It is blessed or unblessed ground; with a multitude of human emotions and pain poured into its earth. In mountain magic, graveyard dirt is a powerful thing. Reverence and fear for the dead seems to be ingrained in all of us.

Some History

Traditional graveyards on family land or churchyards became very overcrowded in America during the mid-1800s. One on the main reasons for the influx of dead was the American Civil War. The Civil War in 1861 became the bloodiest conflict the United States ever faced with over 215,000 dead during its four-year struggle. Many of the dead were brought home and were interred in the church or family burial grounds.

Sicknesses in mountain towns and homesteads were starting to become more common, as the decaying material from buried bodies were beginning to infiltrate the water supplies. Doctors were few in the mountain areas and local healers had their hands full. The creation of cemeteries or burial sites on public land became the solution. Anyone could be buried there.

Though a few community cemeteries go back to the 1600s, it was in the 1800s when city, state and national cemeteries grew. Public cemeteries were designed to be much like a public park, with trees, flowers and shrubs along its walkways. Family plots and above ground tombs dotted the landscape where many people socially met. This was more prevalent in the South where southerners would celebrate days like Flag Day or Decoration Day.

Flag Day became popular after the great war of 1861. The holiday honored those who had fallen. A majority of the southern states fought on the Confederate side. In many of their burial parks, hundreds of small Confederate flags that were placed on soldiers' graves waved in the wind.

Decoration Day was held in the late spring to summer and involved the cleaning of the burial grounds and tombstones. Visiting there to honor the dead also became a social tradition as well. Along with the cleaning of a cemetery, flags and fresh flowers would be placed on graves and in front of tombs. New trees would be planted to honor the people buried there with pomp and ceremony. Many people dressed in their best and brought picnic hampers of food and blankets to have a meal on. Religious services would be held with singing and prayers. It was a time of families getting together to remember those who had died and also to exchange news.

Though these traditions are still honored in many mountain communities today, eventually graveyards and cemeteries reverted back to their true purpose: to bury the dead in a place where one hoped they could rest in peace. The names "graveyard" and "cemetery" became blurred boundaries and most people use both words to describe a burial site whether it is public or private.

The cemeteries or graveyards are known places of spiritual veneration as well as fear, where many believe that spirits abound in their personal city of the dead. The Appalachian tradition of a person wearing black clothing at a funeral was so that the dead would not pay attention to the living. There was a great fear that the dead would whisk the living away with them into the unknown. People also believed that many of the dead would come back either to help family or revenge themselves for any wrong-doings. The dead became part of the night world; filled with spirits, creatures and demons, ready to pounce on anyone not protecting themselves. The graveyards themselves became places of magic and power; where one could make a pact with a devil, god or goddess, or retrieve the dirt from a special grave to cast a spell.

A graveyard is usually a burial ground in a churchyard, though there are many on mountain homesteads. The ground is spiritually sanctified according to belief, making it hard for those of other beliefs to be laid to rest there, if at all. Another common practice was that with many churches, people that committed suicide or were excommunicated were buried outside hallowed ground. Sad. In 1830-31, a cemetery became the designated place of public land for burials as well. - CSB

Gravestones and Markers

Grave markers were used as a location point of a burial in church and family cemeteries. The graves were usually marked with a piece of wood or rough stone to honor the dead and to also keep the newly interred from rising. Sometimes the person's name or initials were inscribed.

By the early 1600s, square-shaped stones of slate or sandstone became popular to mark the site of human burials. Etched with simple designs, the stone's markings would help locate the individual's burial site for visits. Years later, it became common practice to carve or paint on these stones the deceased's name, year of birth and death. Placed at the head of the deceased, gravestones became memorials with symbolic designs describing the last history of the person buried in the ground beneath it, as well as epitaphs or prayers for the protection of their soul. By the mid-1800s, granite became the stone of choice. Headstones made out of iron, bronze or marble were not so common in the mountains.

Some of the earliest symbols carved on the stones reminded us that our passage through life is short and that one should live a good life in order to reach heaven. Hourglasses, skull and crossbones designs, winged cherub heads, urns, picks and shovels of the gravedigger along with biblical scenes, dominated many of the burial grounds. Below is a list of the more common symbols on many North American headstones. Each expressing perhaps the family's hopes for the family member who had passed away, or remembering the age, belief or skills of the one buried beneath the stone.

Symbols representing age:

* **A lamb** - Innocence, a baby

* **An empty chair** - A child

* **A flower bud** - A young child

* **A partially opened flower** - A young adult

* **Broken column** - An early death

* **Butterfly** - Life that was short

* **Flower in full bloom** - Died in the prime of life

* **Shattered urn** - Died of old age; if draped, it means mourning

* **Slain dove** - Premature death

* **Swallow** - A Mother

* **Tree stump** - Life cut short

* **Withered flower blooms or harvested wheat** - a long and full life

Symbols representing types of work:

* **Anvil; Hammer, Anvil, & Crown** together - Symbol of blacksmiths

* **Awl, Knife, & Nippers** - Cobbler or a shoemaker

* **Axe, Knife, & Cleaver** - Butcher

* **Barber Bowl & Razor** - Barber

* **Bees; bees with hive** - Beekeeper

* **Books, with apple or without** - Teacher

* **Brush, scissors, razor or comb** - Hairdresser, Beautician or Barber

* **Caduceus (Two Snakes around Staff)** - Doctor

* **Chisel, mallet and a strip of wood** - Wood carver.

* **Corn, stalk of corn, hoe or plow** - Farmer

* **Even-armed cross with a circle around it** - Red Cross worker

* **Hammer & Square** - Carpenter

* **Hand holding scales or Lady Justice** - Lawyer

* **Loom, Shuttle, & Stretcher** - Weaver

* **Cross, Maltese w/ Firefighter Equipment** - Firefighters

* **Eagle/ US Mail** - United States Postal Service

* **Mortar and Pestle** - Pharmacists

* **Nurse's cap or RN** - Nurse

* **Rake and a spade** - Gardener

* **Scales** - Merchant

* **Stack of Books** - Writer, publisher or seller of books

* **The letter "D" superimposed with Caduceus (rod and two snakes)** - Dentist

* **The letter "V" superimposed with Caduceus (rod and two snakes)** - Veterinarian

* **Wedge & Level** - Mason

U.S. Military

* **Anchor with Crossed Canons** - Confederate States Navy

* **Anchor with Chain or Rope** - United States Navy

* **Anchors, Double with Shield** - United States Coast Guard

* **Anchor, Sextant, & Cross Staff** - Mariner

* **Bee Flying with Gun** - U.S. Navy Seabees

* **Castle** - U.S. Army Corps of Engineers

* **Eagle Clutching Arrows with Shield** - United States Army

* **Globe, Eagle/ Semper Fidelis** - United States Marine Corps

* **Militia Soldier w/ Rifle & 5 Stars** - Army National Guard

* **Wings with Propeller** - U.S. Army Air Corps

* **Eagle with lightning on a shield; Wings with Crest** - U.S. Air Force

Message Symbols

* **Acorns -** Power and authority

* **Anchor** – Hope, steadfast

* **Angel flying** - Resurrection

* **Angel of grief** - Sorrow

* **Anvil** - martyrdom

* **Arch** - Together again in Heaven

* **Arrows** - Mortality

* **Bells & Doves** - Someone married

* **Bellflower** - Gratitude

* **Bible** - Christian

* **Birds** - Flight of the soul

* **Book** - Faith, wisdom

* **Broken chain** - Death of a spouse

* **Broken sword** - Life cut short

* **Lit candle** - Everlasting life

* **Cherub** - Divine

* **Circle, Triangle, and Three Conjoined T's** - Arch mason

* **Column** - A noble life

* **Conch shell** - Wisdom

* **Crescent or Crescent/ Star** - Muslim

* **Cross** - Christianity

* **Cross with flames** - Methodist Religion

* **Cross, anchor and Bible** - Overcoming trials and reward

* **Crossed swords** - Life lost in battle

* **Crown** - Reward and glory

* **Crown with Knight's Head, Crossed Swords, Moon & Stars** - Order of DeMolay

* **Curtains or draped material** - Mourning

* **Daffodil** - Rebirth

* **Dolphin** - Salvation

* **Double arches** - Husband and wife meeting in heaven

* **Dove** - Holy Spirit, Purity

* **Eagles, Double with Pyramid and the Number 32** – 32nd degree Mason

* **Eagle and Shield on Fleur de lis** - The Boy Scouts of America

* **Evergreen** - Eternal life

* **Five Pointed Star with US in the Center and a Wreath** - American Legion

* **Flame** - Flame of life

* **Four Leafed clover** - Four H Club

* **Fruit** - Fruit of life, abundance

* **Garland** - Victory over death

* **Gourds** - Deliverance from grief

* **Grape vine or grapes** - Blood of Christ

* **Hands** - A relation or partnership

* **Hand pointing up** - Direction of heaven

* **Hands clasped** - Farewell

* **Hands holding** - Marriage

* **Hands blessing** - Blessings to those who are left behind.

* **Hands praying** - Prayers to reach heaven

* **Hands with Rosary Beads** - Catholic

* **Harp** - Singing praises

* **Heart** - Devotion; love

* **Horseshoe** - Protection against evil

* **Hourglass (Winged)** - Time; Tempus fugit (Time flies)

* **Inverted Five Pointed Star** - Order of the Eastern Star

* **Ivy** - Faithfulness and memory

* **Lamp** - Immortality

* **Laurel** - Victory, fame, heroism

* **Lily** - Resurrection and purity

* **Lion** - Strength, resurrection

* **Menorah** - Judaism

* **Oak** - Strength

* **Olive branch** - Forgiveness, and peace

* **Open book** - Book of life

* **Palms** - Victory over death

* **Peacock** - The beauty of eternal life

* **Pentagram / Star with Circle** - Wiccan belief

* **Pillow** - To sleep eternally; a deathbed

* **Poppy** - Eternal sleep (Veterans)

* **Rooster** - Awakening, resurrection

* **Scimitar and Five Pointed Star** - The Shriners

* **Shell** - Birth and resurrection

* **Ship** - Voyage across the water; sailing

* **Skeleton** - Life's brevity

* **Skull or Skull & Crossbones** - Death

* **Snake in a circle** - Everlasting life in Heaven

* **Spade or Spade and Shovel crossed** - Death

* **Spinning Wheel over Distaff filled with Flax** - Daughters of the American Revolution

* **Square and Compass** - Freemasonry

* **Star** - Shining light of spirit overcoming death

* **Star of David** - Judaism

* **Swords Crossed** - High ranking military person

* **Sun** - Resurrection

* **Sunrise or Sunset** - Life renewed; life ending

* **Torch** - Death if torch is extinguished; eternal life if upturned

* **Thistles** - Remembrance.

* **Three Links of a Chain** - Grand United Order of Oddfellows

* **Tree trunk** - The beauty of life

* **Triangle** - The Holy Trinity - Truth and equality

* **Trumpets** - Announcement

* **Two, sometimes three holy books** - (either the Bible, Book of Mormon, the Doctrine & Covenants or Pearl of Great Price) - Mormon

* **Urn** - Immortality

* **Weeping willow** - Mourning, sadness and grief

* **Wings with a Parachute and Star** - United States Army Airborne

* **Wreath** - Glory in death

Appalachian Death Beliefs

* Grave decorations are used to keep the spirits of the dead from being restless.

* The coffin of a dead person should line up north to south.

* Many believe that if you touched the dead, it would cure you of sickness.

* Hair of the deceased was sometimes woven and made into memorial jewelry.

* If picture in a frame suddenly falls and breaks, it is a sign of death.

* When someone dies, the closest family member of the deceased will be that last to say farewell.

* If a clock on the wall or mantle hasn't worked for a long time and it suddenly starts ticking, it is warning of impending death.

* Since the 1850s, flowers are placed around a casket to cover the smell.

* Before there were caskets, bodies were wrapped in cloth to be buried. Tree trunks were also used. The body was measured, and the tree trunk cut according to size. It was then hollowed out to put the body in for burial.

* When someone dies in your home, unlock your doors and open your windows to allow the spirit to leave.

* To see an owl at daytime is a sign of death.

* The spirit of the deceased will come back and haunt the family if they do not sit up with the body for the first twenty-four hours after their death.

* Wearing black at funerals keeps the spirits from noticing you and causing harm.

* Don't sweep under a sick person's bed; you may cause them to die.

* If someone dies with their eyes open, shut them as quickly as possible. If not, the deceased could take the person they see with them.

* If a bird flies into your home, it could be a sign of a death in the family.

* The body of the deceased is tied down and covered before the funeral service begins. This ensures that once rigor mortis sets in, the body will not jerk upright during the service.

* **To** "sain" is a Scottish word meaning to make the sign of the cross over or to bless. In a traditional ritual, the oldest woman in the family would wave a lit candle over the body of the dead family member, while making the sign of the cross. This occurs three times. The ceremony concludes once she puts three handfuls of salt in a bowl and places the bowl on the chest of the deceased. This is done to repel any evil why the body lies in state.

* **The** dead person's body can be a witness if they were murdered. Make the accused person touch the body. If it bleeds when they touch it, they are guilty.

* **Carry** the body of the dead out of the house feet first. If not, the corpse's spirit will return to haunt the household.

* **Mountain** folk hope a wind will appear as they take a body out of a house. The wind is supposed to help the person's soul to move on its way.

* **If** a black hound follows you home at night, it means there will be a death of someone close to you.

* **There** is a belief in the mountains that death comes in groups of threes.

* **An** empty rocking chair rocks by itself is a sign of a death.

* **Dogs** howling at night is the sign of a death nearby.

* **A** platter of earth mixed with salt is placed on the chest of the departed during a viewing. It's supposed to symbolize the rejoining of the flesh to the spirit.

* **A** church bell that rings while no one is in the bell tower forewarns that a person in the church's community will die.

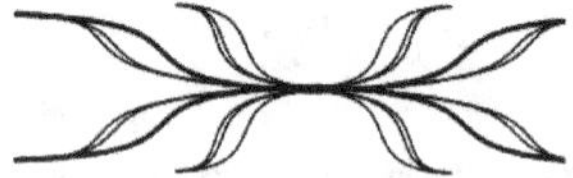

Granny Hagthorn's Bone and Bits Bag

When it came down to others teaching me the ways, Granny Hagthorn was the woman Mam sent me to. She was known around the county for making the best conjure bags and for root working. Mam knew Granny Hagthorn from church and Miss Hagthorn knew me since I was little. She was the one who birthed me. She was always happy to show me things. She just knew I had gifts.

Effie Hagthorn was interested in everything around her. When you went into her cabin, you really didn't know what you might find. A big rag rug was on the front room floor making it warm and comfortable. A big old hornet's nest and a turtle rattle were sitting in a rocking chair by the fireplace. Dried plants hung from the ceiling and bottles of all shapes and sizes filled her shelves with medicines. Another shelf across the room had jars of canned fruits, vegetables and meats. A block of lye soap was sitting on the kitchen table and she was cutting soap before I came in.

At seventy-one, she still helps the other grannies when she can, as an advisor or a fetch and carry. She had started her Granny training at a fairly young age as her mother was a Granny woman, too. Many people come to her because she could fix the things most folks couldn't.

Pulling an old blue enamel pot out, she started to make coffee. "Have a sit, Molly. Just push the block over to the other side of the table. I've got some pie made, too."

"Thanks, Miz Hagthorn. That's a heap of soap. Is all of it for you to use?"

"Nah. I'm makes bags with sweet oil, soap and washcloths to give to my families or anyone else that needs them. They mite need a body clean." Effie Hagthorn's blue eyes twinkled. "Clean home and clean body are good for birthing, too. But enough of that right now. Your Ma believes you are able to see things a little more differently than most. That you might have the sight. She asked me to show you how to make a bone and bits bag."

Looking down at the seat next to me at the table was a burlap sack, tied at the top with thin red and black and white ribbons. There was a faint smell from it of cinnamon and lavender. She had heard stories of Effie Hagthorn and her bag of talking bones and bits. Might powerful things. Now, it was sitting beside her.

The granny woman was busy pouring herself a cup of coffee and filled a jelly glass half full of milk. She then poured a small amount of sweetened coffee into the glass and gave it to the girl.

"After all", the old woman thought, "Molly was only eleven, soon to be twelve. Wish her Ma was feeling better. She would enjoy the visit. Molly's mother had TB and was too sick to leave the county hospital. The girl and her pa are planning to see Julie this evening. I'll give her a call to see how she is. I will make sure to remind Molly to tell her Ma everything we did today."

Sitting the cup and the glass on the table, the woman looked at Molly Buck staring at Effie's bag, and said, "I wouldn't touch them right now; they need to cool off a bit. We just had a man in here that the bones and bits spoke to in a true way. Let them rest until we are ready to take a look at them and I can explain. Let me get the pie."

Chapter II

Molly thought the apple pie and the milky coffee really took the edge off. After washing and drying their plates, she was eager to begin and was curious as to how Granny Hagthorn was able to read so well. Effie put a clean notebook and a newly sharpened pencil in from of Molly at the table.

"Mostly, I just going to show you a few things, being as how you haven't hit moon cycle yet. Your Ma, being sick and all, wanted to make sure you to start learning as soon as possible. I gave her my word. You're going to have to write a heap of this down."

The intense look on Molly's face told the older woman that the girl was ready for her lesson.

And, so it began. The older woman said, "There are five things you need to remember to do when it is time for you to create your bag: 1. Make your own bag and make it out of natural materials. 2. Choose your bones and bits carefully. 3. Connect them to one another in patterns that speak to you. 4. Remember the patterns of how each one connects. 5. The intent of the bag.

Mine is an all-purpose bag; the spirits of the things in it guide me and give me direction when someone comes to ask me a question. A right many call this my conjures bag. I guess it is what it is. This bag is like a piece of myself ; an extension into spirit that gives me the answers I need to know. Once made, people usually put their bags in hidden places. Not me. I keep mine hanging on the wooden post at the top of my bed."

Reaching into the chair, the old woman proudly shows Molly her bag. Worn and old, the brown burlap still held tight. The multi-colored ribbons at the top, cotton.

'What do you mean by 'intent', Granny?" Molly asks.

"Well, some people make bags just for healing and others use their bags just for finding out about love and relationships. And then there are some that use their bags just for locating lost things. Mine is all that and more. Mine can even gossip!"

She took the folded piece of burlap that was with the bag and unfolded it on the table. Painted on the cloth was a cross that went from end to end and a 5-inch circle that went around the area where the four lines met. Each corner of the cloth was marked with a direction; N,S,E,W.

Laughing, she untied the bag with reverence and poured some of the pieces from the bag into the center of the cloth. Out fell a key, a buckeye, a bird's skull with beak and three pieces of cat vertebra joined together. I looked down at the eclectic mix as she kept talking. Smiling at me, the old woman then glanced down at what she had poured out.

"Hmm...they seem to be talking already. They want to make sure I'm teaching you right." She picked them up and put them back in the bag.

The wide-eyed girl shook her head slightly and said, "Yes, Mam," and continued to write.

She told Molly each person's bag carries a number of items that are important to them. Any number chosen has to add up to a double digit (10 or more). As a child, seventeen was her lucky number. She put seventeen pieces in her bag when she got older and made them hers. Seventeen is a highly spiritual number. The number could represent the door to the universe opening wide and bringing hope, opportunity and deliverance. But there is also another side to this number. Added together the one and the seven, it equals an eight. Eight is the number of Karma or one's true fate. It can also represent the results of hard work or struggle.

"So yes, the bones will speak to you of your dreams and tell what may be up for you in the upcoming future," Hagthorne explained. "But they also reveal truths and speak of the fates of you and others. My bag took me two years to make. I carefully chose each piece."

Along with the pieces she had already pulled out, there also was:

A white poker chip with an "X" on one side and an "O" on the other

A piece of coyote jaw

A raccoon penis bone or baculum

A jingle bell

A large pearl button, about an inch wide

A small shell with the number "3" written on it

A heart shaped bead

A tiny miniature bird

One die (dice)

A token coin

A turkey wish bone

A rattlesnake rattle

Dried rosebuds tied together

A silver dime

Here is what each bone or bit means in her workings:

Key - Opening doors, the source, belonging to a group or organization

Buckeye - Luck or fortune

One die (dice) - Fate, purpose and direction. Luck and gambling.

Bird skull – Mystery, hidden things, passing secrets

Cat vertebra (backbones) - Backing up to analyze, waiting for the right moment to step forward.

A small shell with the number "3" written on it. - Shell is water and emotion. Three, the number of change and growth. Perhaps a change in a personal relationship, could also be a normal pregnancy period.

Jingle bell - Announcements or warnings.

Large pearl button - Intuition or dreams

Piece of Coyote jaw – Trickery, avoidance in getting something done.

X and O poker chip - Yes "X" and no "O"; life "X "or death "O"

Rattlesnake rattle - Dangerous and dark. Aggressive sexually

Heart shaped bead - The heart; a love relationship

Token coin - Wasted time, unreal

Silver dime - Fortune and gain

Turkey wish bone - Wishes coming true

3 Tied dried rosebuds - Romance leaning towards love.

Raccoon penis bone (baculum) - Sexual attraction

Collecting up most of the pieces she had showed me, she left some of them on the cloth and repositioned them. As a training exercise, the old woman asked me to pretend that a woman comes to her for help dealing with a new love relationship. She has me picture this woman shaking the bag and having Miz Hagthorne takes the bag from her and pour out the pieces on the cloth. As she is telling this story to me, she points at each bit or bone on the cloth that explained the answer.

This is what I saw: the pieces that clustered the most together from the bag, landed close to the center. This, I learned, means that you need to look at the whole situation. Grouped together was the poker chip with "o" facing up, the piece of coyote jaw, the jingle bell, raccoon penis bone and silver dime; off to the side closest to the woman asking the question, were the token coin and the rosebuds lying together. The rest of the pieces were scattered into the four directions. What are these clusters of bones and bits telling the woman? Does this woman have a good relationship according to the throw?

"Molly, what do you think? Watch this as I show it to you."

"Her new love is not what he seems (she points at the coyote jaw). I would tell her not to get too involved with him emotionally until she knew him better ("O" chip). She's been given a warning (jingle bell). She needs to watch and observe. Is he a hard worker? Or, is he hanging around and having her do the work for him (silver dime)? Is he known to be an honest man (coyote jaw)? She sees him in a romantic way (rosebuds next to woman), but (the token coin) is also with the flowers. The spirits might be telling her that he may not be as interested in her as she is in him. He may just want to be sexually physical with her (baculum bone, raccoon penis bone) and nothing more."

Single pieces that fall in directional areas: These are used for advice depending upon which area the pieces fell (N, S, E or W). An example would be that the die (dice) has landed alone in the West. The advice could be that she is taking a chance to become emotionally involved in the relationship and that she needs to observe and follow her gut.

Molly wrote furiously to keep up with her. Finally, she said, "Now remember; when it is your time to do so: Make your own bag, pick a personal number of things to add to your bag; at least ten or more. Design and make you own ritual cloth, too. Make sure the pieces relate to you, so you will have a connection to each piece. Work with the pieces you have a bit each day and let them tell you stories when you ask questions like the example above. You can ask stuff you already know to see if they are giving you true answers. Eventually, they (the spirits) will talk to you. One more thing:

At night before bed, you will hold the bag with the bones and bits to your heart and say, 'And me, with thee.' Sleep with the bag for 28 days before you use it on others."

The old woman slowly picked up her pieces and put them in her bag. Then, she asked if I had any more questions. I shook my head no.

"Then I will bid you good evening, my Mollie." The girl packed up her things and headed for home.

****

Making a bag for your Bones or Bones and Bits

A bone or bone and bits bag are a powerful tools of divination. Put together with thoughtful consideration, the pieces are known to spiritually "speak", giving the reader the answers they seek. It is best to create your bag on a full moon, to draw good energy. Because all the pieces in the bag are personal symbols belonging to the reader, the bag must be kept close at hand. Bone or bone and bits readers have been known to hang it over their beds for protection. Rub oil or herbs on the bags to "feed" the spirits that live in the bag. It will make the bag more powerful.

You're going to need roughly around four feet of cloth and two feet of cotton cord. This length of cloth should make you a divination bag big enough to carry all your materials (even odd sizes) that you can cast, as well as a cloth for casting them on. Use natural materials such as burlap or cotton. Start by cutting around roughly two feet of the material and set it aside. This will be used for making the bag. The remaining material will be used for making the casting cloth. You can sew the bag and the casting cloth on a sewing machine, but you put more of your own energy and intention into it by sewing it by hand. Your intention is important.

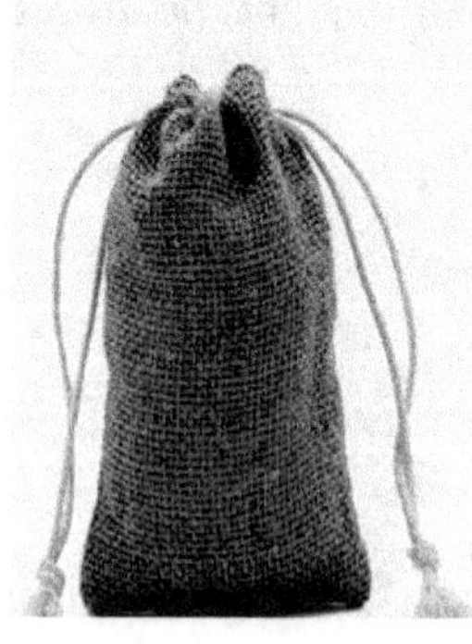

As you sew, focus in on the purpose of what you need to make these tools for. Use red thread if you can. Make sure the bag is made with a draw string attached. You can do this by folding the mouth of the bag ¼ inch over and sewing. An easy way to thread the cord through is to put a small safety pin on one end of your cord then thread it through and tie off the ends. Once the bag is completed, put it to one side.

Then, measure the rest of the material, then cut from it another 3x4 foot square piece. A cross- shaped design should be drawn or stitched across it, creating four even areas. The cross will hold your direction; mark the letter of the direction in each square: North (physical form, money or things), South (spiritual, creative, sexual) East (mental thought or ideas), West (Initiation into new things, emotional, intuitive); the center area represents things what need to be quickly addressed.

Most of these cloths are very plain but if you want, you can add whatever magical designs you feel you need. Put the finished materials (folding the square in the bag) under your pillow and sleep with it for three nights.

The type of bones used in your bag can be anything symbolic to you. They are believed to be a bridge that connects the bone reader with spirits or their ancestors. A raven skull could possibly represent mystery, magic or sight. A raccoon penis bone could be sex or desire. Possum bones are sometimes painted with designs. The shape may connect something within you more than what the actual bones are. Note: Make sure all bones are properly cleaned and dried before adding to pouch. This also goes for any organic materials.

Bones can be used in their natural form, painted by color, or have symbols drawn or painted on them. What other things can you put in a bone bag besides bones? Holey stones, coins, seed pods such as nutmeg or a High John root, keys, feathers, shells, dice or medallions; heart-shaped things, too. Anything as long as it isn't breakable when thrown onto the cloth. That will be up to you.

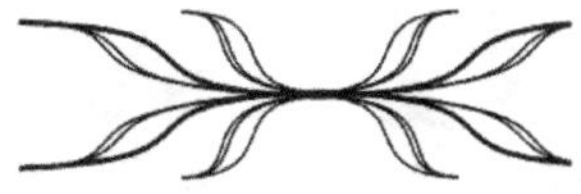

Mountain Witches

A witches' power is said to bc truly supernatural. In mountain folklore, she becomes the shapeshifter or skin-walker with abilities to change the winds. She can pass through keyholes even when the doors are locked. Entering her home, the witch takes the scarf from her head and shakes or wrings it out over her kitchen table. From within its hidden folds, would tumble out all sorts of things that she had stolen from others that day.

Three major cultures have laid bare their tracks through the Appalachians and created a way of life rich with history and beliefs. Fascinating tales of monsters, spirits and magical beings appeared in the mountain regions even before the 1700s, when European settlers came to the Appalachians looking for fertile land and freedom. Though some stories are said to be only Cherokee, African or European, many who look for the origin of any of these particular beliefs, cannot normally find them. This is due to the secluded societies and intermarriage that brought together tales of witches and magical people from the Old World and the New.

Told late at night was one of many tales featuring an evil shapeshifter-witch by the name of **Spearfinger**. Spearfinger was known to have a long first finger that was sharp and shaped like a knife. She would travel about the countryside, disguising herself as a kindly, elderly woman. Gaining the trust of the children she met, she would lead them to their doom.

This witch's origin is said to be Cherokee, but the Germans who settled in the area also have folk stories about **drudes**, who are said to be witches or evil spirits who appear in the shape of old hags who carried knifes under their aprons and would capture and eat children. The story of **Hansel and Gretel** in ***Grimm's Fairy Tales*** is an example.

Powerful witches and healers in the mountains used African root working and Hoodoo blended with German Powwow. Sympathy magic and the veneration of ancestors in the African tradition were used to cure ailments, defend oneself from curses and to achieve power and control over a situation. Conjuring- to use spells to bring about a connection between the spell work and the spiritual being and Hoodoo, which uses training in religious prayer and practical skills.

In Native legends, witches had the ability to become invisible to most. Only gifted medicine men of the tribe could see them and would protect the sick or dying from having their heart or their liver taken. Mountain witches were notorious for stealing and eating the liver of people they encountered. Their desire was to consume the soul inside and live one year longer than the normal lifespan of the liver eaten. The heart and the liver were known to house the human soul in many cultures.

Last, but not least is the village witch, wise woman or granny witch. Traditional roots lead back to African, German, Scotch-Irish or Welsh origins. In villages or family groups, the women cooked and farmed while the men hunted. Working with the plants, trees and soil as well as connecting to the all the other natural world around them, gave many women a hands-on education that is passed down through the generations and taught to gifted family members. In the Appalachians, Grannies or Granny witches became the communities' healers, midwives and leaders. Simple, tried but true techniques were looked upon with magical wonder.

"The Old Witch" (Mrs. Alice Downey) by Nancy Ford Cones, ca. 1923

* In the mountain communities, medicine people and witches are still respected, but are also feared. Much of what they have taught themselves was unknown by many. Time and understanding perfects the craft.

* Modern witchcraft and pagan beliefs have grown from this fertile history

Witch Folklore

* The coins in your pocket will turn black if you kiss a witch.

* Mix pawpaw in a person's tobacco to find out if they are a witch. It will make them sick.

* Build a baby's cradle from rowan wood to protect it from witches.

* Drive three iron nails in the front door of your house to keep a witch out.

* Tie a red bag around an animal to un-bewitch them.

* Feed a person salty food to see if they are a witch. Witches cannot eat a lot of salt and will

   loudly complain.

* Put a bible under the bed of the person believed to be a witch. They will not be able to sleep on

   the bed if they are.

* Do not plant an elder tree by your house. Not only is it bad luck, but a witch may live inside the

   tree.

* Never make a cradle out of elder wood. A witch could have access to your baby. Mountain

   people had to use caution as some types of elder can look like rowan wood, which was used as

   a protection from witchcraft.

* Scratch a cross under the chair of someone you think is a witch. They will not be able to sit in

   the chair if they are.

* Never start a fire using elder wood. It will cause a witch or a spirit to become angry.

* Lighting a piece of Mullein in your house or while doing a working is said to keep bad witches

   at bay. Another name for mullein is Hag's Taper.

* Juniper bushes are planted by the front of the house to keep witches away. It's said that a witch

   could not enter unless she was able to count all the needles on the bush. Bunches of fennel

   hung by doors and windows are protection as well.

* Burn Wood Betony with uncrossing incense for spell breaking.

Knotwork, Poppets and Corn Dollies

Fertility is traditionally tied with grass knots and made into dolls to protect the fields.

Appalachian farms were once very isolated from cultural towns and cities. People living in the mountains relied upon the farmers' harvest each season, as well as the use of hunting, fishing and local wildcrafting. The harvest bonded the farmer and the people to the land. Ritual sacrifice and fertility rituals were used for growing things that were brought over from other countries. Being adaptable, they also used the traditional Native American techniques of farming and breeding.

Knotwork

Knotwork binds or releases spells. The origin of this folk magic originated from the first peoples who sailed the seas, settled on the land and farmed the earth.

Cords or ribbons of various colors are braided together, and a written spell or rhyme is repeated while concentrating on your intent. Then the cord is consecrated (using water, air, earth or fire elements) and blessed.

Cord Colors:

White - Pure and innocent, beginnings

Black - Binding and boundaries, darkness

Yellow or gold - Sun; magic of the sun, realization

Silver - Moon; Moon magic, reflections and dreams

Red - Passion; blood, Mars energy, fire

Blue – Spirituality, peace

Brown – Earth, animals, things of value

Purple – Mystery, hidden, astral travel

Orange - Life force, talents, energy

Pink – Romance, gentleness

Green – Nature, growth, abundance

Gray – Integration, neutral

To strengthen any spell working, use items such as stones, feathers, beads, charms, herbs, flowers, hair or any object you feel gives it power that can be tied into the knots. Repeat the words (see below) as you knot until completed, or you can write your own spell expressing your desires for your knot work. Having a rhythm or rhyme to what you write, helps build the energy along with your desire and intentions. This classic spell below is an example.

Spell of the Cord

By the knot of one, the spell's begun

By the knot of two, I will it true

By the knot of three, so shall it be

By the knot of four, its strength is more

By the knot of five, so may it thrive

By the knot of six, the spell is fixed

By the knot of seven, the power of

heaven

By the knot of eight, they all relate

By the knot of nine, the spell is mine.

Poppets

Sympathetic magic is still being used. The concept of creating something with an intent or purpose is used to bring about a mirrored affect. Many use poppets as a type of spell casting. This is done by creating an image of the person and then giving it a name. It is believed that whatever is done to this magical likeness will affect the person it represents. Useful for spells that can attract a lover, they are also used for healing, as well as for directing negative energy towards a person. Poppets or dolls can also be used for banishing spells.

Images can be made out of clay, wax, wood or cloth; some people even use pipe cleaners. Poppets made out of cloth are usually filled with herbs or dirt that are needed for that particular spell. Personal items are added to tie the subject of the spell to the doll. Different things, such as paper or cloth cutouts, candle wax, knotted cords, photographs, drawings, written lists, pins or nails can be applied as a spell is chanted.

Healing Poppets

Cut out a man-shaped form from two pieces of white or natural cloth. If there is more than one problem that needs healing, you can attach a small paper or cloth swatch of the proper color to the area that needs to be healed. You can also place a written request inside the poppet. This work should be done either on the new or full moon for positive healings and workings.

Healing Colors and Herbs

Colored cloth swatches:

Blue (spiritual, emotional)

Green (physical growth)

Orange (life, vitality)

Yellow (mental health, mental agility and perception)

Here are some types of wild or garden grown herbs you can use for stuffing: **Echinacea, Rosemary, Allspice, Yarrow, Balm of Gilead, Chamomile, Thistle, Cinquefoil, Eucalyptus, Ginseng, Peppermint, Spearmint, Thistle, Garlic, Yarrow, Aloe Vera and Lavender.**

Sew the doll together leaving the head open so you can fill the form.

Select three healing herbs, along with any personal items (hair, nails, etc.) of the sick person or any requests.

As you stuff the poppet with the ingredients, say:

"Herbs to trees to roots and flowers

Gather healing and give it power

In the name of the Father, Son and Holy

Ghost."

As you sew it shut, repeat:

"Herbs to trees to roots and flowers

Gather healing and give it power

In the name of the Father, Son and Holy

Ghost."

While holding the poppet in both hands and picturing the sick person in your mind, say for the last time:

"Herbs to trees to roots and flowers

Gather healing and give it power

In the name of the Father, Son and Holy

Ghost.

Amen."

Place the poppet in an area that is sunny and has access to fresh air.

Love spell using Poppets

This spell uses two poppets. If you are using cloth to make them, cut each form out of two pieces of the material and sew them together with pink, white or red thread (use these colors of cloth, too, if you have them). Take a few moments while you are cutting and sewing to think of the person each poppet is being made for. Leave an opening at the top to fill the doll with at least three different kinds of herbs aligned with the planet Venus. Use a red candle wax or red paper hearts, as well as any nail clippings or hair that you found of that person. Any scrap material inside the doll with body fluids on them makes it even more powerful. If you do not have these, a picture of the person or some of their hand writing will suffice. Best time to do this spell is when the moon is starting to wax towards a half moon (1st quarter; attraction energy is strong)/full moon.

As you sew each of these poppets shut, say three times:

"Made to form

I give you life

Your body to (her or his) body

Your breathe to (her or his) breathe

Passion to passion

Bonded to _____ and for _____

I name you __________

By hearts entwined, come love to thee."

Tie them together facing each other with a piece of red ribbon and place in a box with rose petals.

Keep the box under the bed where you sleep.

**** Herbs ruled by Venus:**

Rosemary, Rose petals or buds, Verbena, Cinnamon, Yarrow, Catnip, Lavender, Patchouli, leaves from Strawberries, Valerian, Jasmine, Vervain or Ginger can be added.

Though most cunning folk only heal, there are those in the mountains who use images to write a wrong.

Poppet used to reverse a wrong done to you by someone else

Fill this poppet with graveyard dirt and rosemary, parsley or sage. You can also add nails, pins, thorns, a button from a shirt the person wore, hair, nail clippings, a photo, a used handkerchief belonging to the person, any kind of tissue or cloth with that person's body fluid on it, or something they have written on. Rope or cord is used for binding, hanging or knotting the effigy. Do this on a waning or dark moon. Sew the form together while thinking of the person.

Hold it in both hands and say:

> **Made to this form I give you life**
>
> **This body (the poppet) to your body**
>
> **This breathe (person working the magic blows air on the poppet) to your breathe**
>
> **This blood (a drop from the wronged party) to your blood**
>
> **I name you __________**
>
> **Mine to use when the time of judgment comes.**

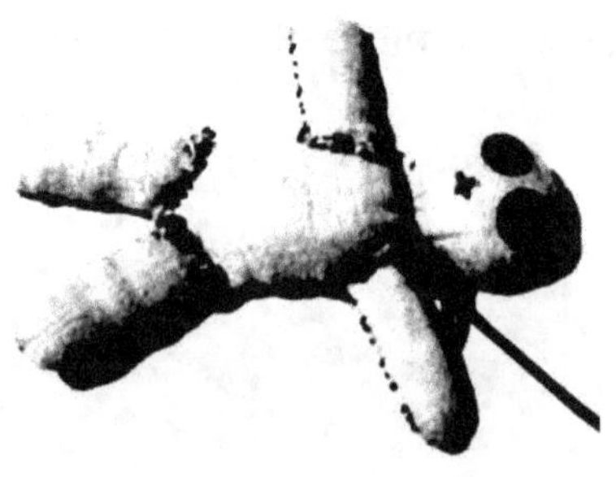

Corn Dollies

Ancients believed that the spirits of the grain would be without a home once their community's fields were harvested. The corn dolly was made to be a comfortable shelter for these spirits until the following spring.

Agricultural fertility magic varies in different farming regions. Some rural communities called for the oldest woman who had birthed children herself, to create the corn dolly. She was given the title, "Corn Mother." Other farming areas use the youngest mature female member, who though grown, was still a virgin. She was known as a "Corn Maiden."

The women who accepted these titles were responsible for the last corn sheaves left in the community's field at the end of harvest. These sheaves were made into a corn dolly which took the form of a Maiden (good year) or a Crone (bad year). The dolly would be kept in their homes until the following Spring.

The Corn Mother or Maiden returns to the fields on the first day of planting. A small procession follows behind her. Carrying the dolly back to the field from where she had gotten her last husks, she then buries it. The dolly would be ploughed back into the field or burned. If burned, the ashes would be spread on the field.

Seed saved from the previous autumn was planted and the cycle would begin once more. Grain (corn is one type of grain) symbolizes death and rebirth.

How to Make Corn Husk Dolls

Materials: Scissors, bowl of water (warmed) to soak, soften and make husks pliable if dry; if fresh, green corn husk from a corn cob (about a dozen pieces should be plenty), twine

Directions: Take 4 pieces of husk and make all of them even-edged at the top. Take about 3 inches of twine and tie them tightly together about an inch and a half down the husk. Then, with your scissors, round off the edges. Turn it upside-down so that it looks like a big paintbrush in your hand. Fold those long pieces down and over the area you tied off. This creates the head of the doll. Shape with your hands and tie it off with twine.

To make the arms of the doll, take another piece of husk and roll it tightly. Tie off each end with a piece of twine. Slide it through the loose husk under the head/neck area. Tie twine around the middle of the loose husks to form a waist. Take a strip of husk and wrap around the neck in a crisscross pattern in the front of the doll to form the shoulders. Then, take 5 pieces of husk (even at the top) and place them around the "waist" of the doll. Tie off both the top and bottom pieces with one piece of twine. This creates a "dress" effect.

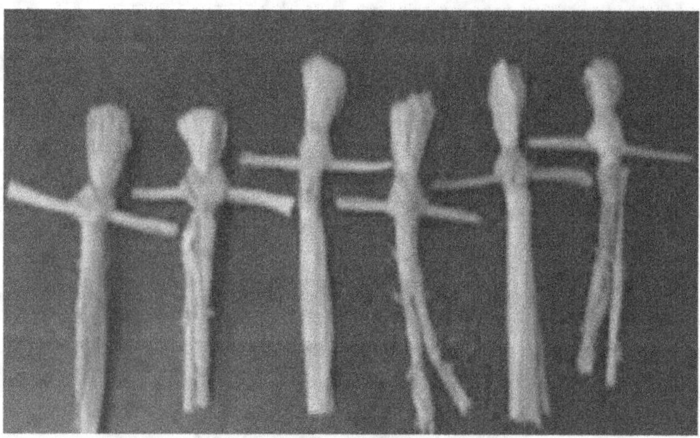

Dolls can have faces drawn or painted on and dressed in clothes or left simple.

Love Spells and Sexual Allure

By Earth, Air, Water and Fire

Grant me all the love I desire

One of our strongest desires is to be loved. Many men and women of all ages feel that a little extra "oomph" should be used to get their wishes fulfilled. They turn to magic with hopes that they can lead happy lives with the ones they love. The moon's cycle is important to their requests, adding energy good or bad.

> **New Moon** - Washes away the bad
>
> **Waxing Moon** - Desire is drawn when the moon is Wax
>
> **Waning Moon** - Clears the way; disruption and destruction are done
>
> **Full moon and its silver light** - Love, abundance and money

Simple Love Spells

Want your lover to come back?

*Find his footprint impressions on the ground and take a spoonful of dirt from them. Mix the dirt with a pinch of chopped basil and a few drops of your urine. Make into a small ball and let dry. Bury it by the steps of the door your lover would come through on a night during waxing moon. Your lover will return.

* Boil the foot of a goose and give the water to the person you really like.

* Is your lover honest and true? Put a little salt in his shoe and then ask him.

* Carry apricot pits to attract love.

* Steal some of your lover's wash water. Soak a piece of red lace in it. Make sure the piece of lace is long enough to tie a knot in it. Lay the lace out to dry. Wait for a waxing moon that is in your favor for this type of knot magic. Holding it in your hands, think about the two of you together. When you have a clear picture in your mind, call out to him, and tie the knot. Keep the knot in your pillowcase and your lover will return to you.

* Take an unwashed sock of yours and one of your lover's. Tie them together and throw the socks under the bed. Keep them there; he will not stray.

*On a full moon, take a whole hot pepper and a straight pin. Draw a heart on the pepper with the pin and inscribe your lover's initials and his birth date in the center. Stick the pin through the heart's center and say, "Only my heart can heal your heart. Only my love is your desire." Put it in a pink pouch and bury it outside your door or hide it underneath the mattress where you and your lover will lie. The person you desire will think only of you.

*Take a small wooden box and rub the insides with "Come to Me "oil. Then place a raccoon penis bone, a red paper heart with his name on it, a piece of red Jasper and a picture of you. Place the box in the back of your underwear drawer. Your lover will always desire you and will not stray.

* Take an apple and core it out. On a small piece of paper, write the name of the person you desire. Plug the bottom of the apple, leaving the top open. The plug can be made from a piece of soft wax, chewing gum you or your lover has chewed, or a chunk of the leftover bottom core. Place the paper inside the core of the apple. Then, pour a small amount of honey on top of it and seal the top. Place the apple in a small brown paper bag and leave it to sit overnight. Put it in a place where insects cannot get to it. The next morning bury the bag by your doorstep. This should sweeten someone's (the name on the paper) thoughts about you and draw them close.

* Use yarrow flowers in marriage and love charms to keep someone faithful.

* Sugar is used the same way as honey to sweeten a person or a situation. Take a small, clean plastic food container (one with a lid) and place your lover's picture in the bottom of it. Pour an inch of the sugar on top of the picture. Seal the container and place it on the top shelf of your kitchen cabinet. Your sweetheart will come to you for comfort and love.

* Make two dollies out of a burlap bag. Sew them with red thread and fill them with Venus herbs. One should have some personal item of yours inside (hair, nail clippings, tissue with any type of body fluid or photo). The other should have one or more personal items of the person you desire. Cut out a double-heart in pink paper and place it between the two soft bodies of the dolls and then tie them together. They should be tied face to face. You can use a piece of cord or a necklace chain that belongs to you. You can also anoint with any love or attraction oil you want. Place in a cloth draw-string bag and put it up someplace safe in your home where it can be close to you.

* Verses from the KJB from the Songs of Solomon are used in making love oils, powders, baths and spells. This verse is great to use in sugar spells for sweetness and passion.

"Let him kiss me with the kisses of his mouth: for thy love is better than wine.

Because of the savour of thy good ointments thy name is as ointment poured forth, therefore do the virgins love thee.

Draw me, we will run after thee: the king hath brought me into his chambers: we will be glad and rejoice in thee, we will remember thy love more than wine: the upright love thee." Songs of Solomon

Chapter 1- 2:4(KJB)

The Charmed and Spellbound

Anything can be used to create a spell. Spells for love use things associated with romance such as: herbs and colors, candles, hearts, hair and body fluids, photos, written requests, sweetening things like honey and sugar; shells, perfume and the smells of incense smoke are just some of these. Most workings are done in the waxing or full cycle of the moon.

*Take a piece of bread, one tablespoon of honey, small piece of paper and a pen, a toothpick and your house key. Press the key into the bread. The impression of the key should be made three times on the same side of the bread so that the marks cover most of the slice. Spread out the honey across the impressed bread. Then take a small piece of paper (about1by 2 inches) and write your lover's name on it. Place the paper with his written name in the center of the honeyed bread and fold the bread up three times. Take a wooden toothpick and push it through the bread to hold it together. Bury the bread under a honeysuckle bush on a full moon.

Awakening Love and Passion

* The root of the trillium or wake-robin is known as "Dixie John" and is used to make a love oil.

* Use honeysuckle flowers for "sweetening" spells.

* If you wish to dream of a lover take two bay leaves and put them in your pillow case before you go to sleep.

* A rose's sensual smell can lower anxiety when having sex.

* Men carry buckeyes in their pockets to improve their sexual power, attract money and can help cure rheumatism.

* Grind the petals of wild roses and orrisroot together. Sprinkle the powder on the sheets of your lover will lie. It will keep them from straying.

* Cinnamon, when used regularly, lowers blood sugar and increases sex drive.

* Place a piece of ivy under your pillow before bed and you will dream of your true love.

* Seeing a white dove flying over your house is an omen of a marriage at the homestead within one year.

* Use bluebells in your spells for faithfulness.

* Make a heart with apple blossoms and pink wax melted together. Keep it in a small bag in your drawer. It will attract love.

* Vanilla's scent is sensual, and relaxing. Used in "Come to Me" spells.

* Hang an apple peel outside your front door on the day of a full moon. The first person through your door, is said to have the same initials as the person who you will love.

* Jasmine's sweet scent attracts both men and women and can spark passion.

* Damiana has aphrodisiac effects. It stimulates blood flow to the genital area and increasing sensitivity.

* Damiana and Saw Palmetto made into a tonic is used for male prostate health.

* Wear around your neck a "mountain toothpick" to attract love. The "toothpick" is made from a raccoon penis bone.

* Take some leaves of myrtle and throw it into the fireplace. The face of your future husband should appear.

* If a woman gives a man a fresh shoot of basil and he keeps it, he will love her forever.

* Plant lavender and roses outside your front door to attract love.

Herbs Used in Spell Work for Love or Passion

Balm of Gilead Buds - Used to heal relationships

Bergamot - Love and attraction

Cardamom Seed - For sexual passion

Catnip - Sex

Cherry Bark - For attraction

Cinnamon - For attraction; money too

Coriander Seed - Faithfulness and love

Cumin Seed - Steadfast love

Damiana - Lust

Deer's Tongue - For marriage proposals

Fennel - Fertility and love

Gentian Root - Love drawing

Ginger - Hot sex

Honeysuckle Flowers - Binds your lover to you

Hyssop - Forgiveness

Jasmine Flowers - Dreams involving love

Jupiter Berries - Boosts sex drive

Lavender Flowers - Love

Lovage Root - Passion

Patchouli - Love and money

Raspberry Leaf - Love that doesn't stray

Red Clover - Happy marriage

Rose - Love

Skullcap - Faithfulness in marriage

Star Anise - Healing and building strong bonds

Violet Leaf - Love

Vanilla - Romantic love

Critters and Creatures

Just think, on a dark night, you might just hear a-rattling and a-bumping.

Spirits Haunt the Trails and Byways

* Those who have hiked the trails up through Grandfather Mountain in Linville, North Carolina, tell of tales of walking spirits. Thought their purpose is unknown, these ghostly images intent upon reaching their destination in the unknown distance, ignore those they pass by. They are usually dressed in clothing of another time and walk the hikers on the trail without a word or sound. They are known to disappear before others can turn towards the direction of their passing.

* Big Ridge State Park is located in Maynardville, Tennessee. This 3,687-acre park is located on the Appalachian Ridge and Valley mountain range. Walkers and hikers are apprehensive of some of the known pathways in the area, especially around Norton Cemetery and the land where the old Matson Hutchinson homestead once stood. It's said that cries for help are heard from the ghost of Hutchinson's daughter, who died of tuberculosis sometime in the 1800s. Pictures taken in the old cemetery seem to have unearthly shadows or silhouettes that stand behind some of the gravestones.

* Mount Chocorua is located in The White Mountain National Forest of New Hampshire. It is here that that spirit of Chocorua had been sighted. Chocorua was an American Indian who once had a homestead on the mountain. The story goes that he came home one day to find that his son had died and Chocorua believed his neighbor had poisoned him. Wanting revenge, the Native American man killed the neighbor's family. Chocorua was pursued by his neighbors up the mountain in an attempt to capture him. Rather than be trapped and hung, he cursed both the mountain's settlers and the trail they pursued him on, jumping off the mountain to his death.

* Mammoth Cave in Kentucky was once used as a living space and hospital for tuberculosis patients from 1842-1843. The skeleton-like patients were seen walking around in hospital gowns through the passageways by people visiting the cave. The constant sound of hollow coughing echoed through the cave system. Most of the patients died there and their bodies were laid among the rocks in the side chamber. Many who visit the cave still claim to hear the ghostly choking and coughing of those who had died.

Black Dog, Old Shuck and the Hellhound

Standing seven foot tall and dark as night, this creature looks at you with blood red eyes that are the size of dinner plates. Known throughout the British Isles as The Black Dog or Old Shuck, sightings have been historically documented. The most famous incident takes place in the 1500s. In 1577, at Saint Mary's Church in England, a huge black dog entered the building during a dramatic thunderstorm and killed two people. The creature became known in legend as a harbinger of death. It was believed, if seen, the person seeing it or one of the person's relatives may die within a year.

The name Shuck comes from an Old English word, "scucca," meaning a devil or fiend. It is said that he walks with no sound and its mournful howling can freeze you with fear. The creature brings with it a deep feeling of despair and sadness before he is actually seen. This legend has been carried across the water and into the mountain regions of the eastern and southern United States by Europeans that had settled there.

Reports of sightings in the Appalachians usually associated the black dog with the crossroads. Here, he becomes the Devil Dog, Hellhound or the Snarly Yow, whose ghostly figure disappears in a bright flash of light and leaves behind scorched marks and the smell of brimstone. He is a shapeshifter and hunter from Hell known to track down the sinful.

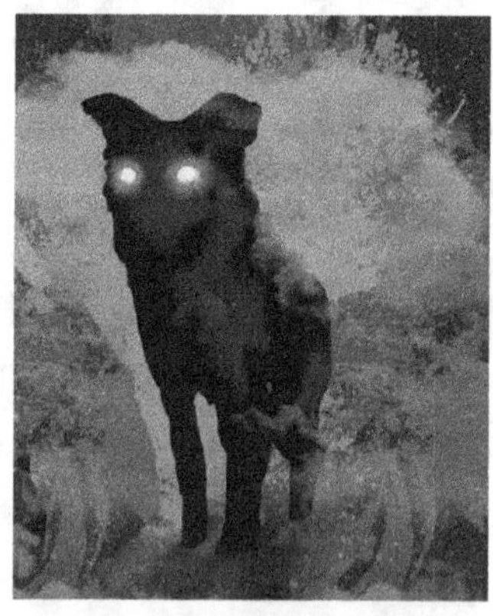

Fairies

Many native tribes in the Appalachians had stories of these supernatural beings; with the Cherokee stories the most well-known. Little People were thought by the Cherokee to be the builders of an ancient, long wall that snakes up through the Appalachians from Georgia. Called "Nunnehi", they are the immortal spirits that live on the land. The many stories told about them have no origin group, as both European and Native stories are similar. Mountain belief states that if a mortal person had children with a Nunnehi or Fairy being, then the children born of that union would sight-gifted or become a great healer.

Scotch-Irish and Irish settlers that came to the new American continent also brought their tales of the Good Folk or the Little People. These beings or "Fairies" are said to bless a wandering traveler or curse those who are caught in acts of cruelty. Some are shapeshifters, known to take human babies and replace them with one of their own. Many problems with farm livestock were blamed on them.

True to belief, the many mountain families have born within them, people with special insights or abilities. A gift given to their families by otherworldly beings. So, if you are in a woodland area and are able to sit quietly by a mountain stream or river, you may still be able to hear their laughter and the faint strains of music.

The Moon-Eyed People

With pure white skin and their inability to see in the daylight, the big-eyed, mountain-dwarfed race that lived in the caves and underground caverns in the western Appalachians, were observed and written about in the late 1700s. There is a good possibility that the "Moon-Eyed" people were indeed human and had adapted themselves over the generations, to survive in the cave system. Their bodies and eyesight changed with their darker cave environments.

Legends speak of the remains found of a group of Welsh soldiers who ended up living in the mountain caverns around Murphy, North Carolina. Sightings from backwoods people living in the area said that these cavern people were deformed, and they fled from the light.

Stories go that cave dwellers and the local Indians were constantly bickering. One night, when the full moon became bright, a band of Creek or Cherokee Indians ambushed the cave dwellers, forcing them from their home and scattering what was left of the survivors into parts unknown. Many of the cave survivors were said to have escaped towards the Kentucky side of the Appalachians, where the coal seams are. Legends say they are still being sighted in old mines and backwood cave areas.

Mermaid Point

During the Revolutionary War era, there were sightings of mermaids on a sandbar at the junction of Deep River and Haw River, in an area called Mermaid Point in Guilford County, North Carolina. The mermaids had been sighted around two o'clock in the morning by people leaving Ambrose Ramsey's tavern. Legend states that the mermaids came from the sea to use the fresh water to wash the salt out of their hair. In the 1900s, a dam was built in the area that flooded the tavern as well as the sandbar. There have been no sightings since.

Mothman

Gravediggers in Clendenin, West Virginia reported a sighting of a winged man-like creature that silently flew over their heads while they were preparing to dig a grave. It had eyes like coals. This creature is considered a harbinger of disaster. Multiple sightings were witnessed just before the collapse of the Silver Bridge in Pleasant Point, West Virginia in 1967.

The Yahoo

A type of Bigfoot or Skunk ape, the six to seven foot tall, reddish-brown, hairy man-like creatures are known to be very aggressive and territorial. These crypto-animals can be heard through the West Virginia mountains at night. Their call, similar to the word, "Yahoo!" "Yahoo!" along with a series of whistles and clicks. They are said to make their nests in caves and trees.

The Dwayyo

Germans that settled in the Appalachians, brought with them legends of the Hexenwolf, a man-wolf who attacked, killed and devoured people traveling through wooded countryside. The Hexenwolf, Dwayyo and the Maryland Dog Man seem to be the same creature. The Dwayyo's first recorded sighting occurred in 1944 in Fredrick County in Maryland. A cross between a wolf and a human, this massive nine-foot monster was seen fleeing through the woods screaming into the night. Many had claimed to have seen its footprints. Outbreaks of sightings were known to occur during rabies season.

The Snallygaster

Though there have been sightings in the southeastern mountains of North America since the 1700s, by 1908, the Smithsonian Institute announced it was offering to pay a reward for the capture or skin of this creature. This came about when several newspapers reported a sighting in Preston County, West Virginia and had eye-witness reports. Known also as a Schneller Geist (quick spirit) by German immigrants that came to the Appalachian Mountains to settle, it is described as a demonic half lizard, half bird, having an alligator-like head with a beak filled with razor-sharp teeth and long talons. With its twenty to thirty foot wingspan, it has been known to quickly and silently fly down and steal livestock. Some reports state the creature sucks blood.

The Hopkinsville Goblins (Kentucky)

It was August 21, 1955, when a group of adults with children came into the Hopkinsville police station to complain that they were attacked in their home by aliens from another planet. Having to hold them off with gunfire for almost four hours, the dozen or so space aliens that had attacked them were described as being three to four feet tall with a face that lacked any distinct facial features. They went on to say that the creatures had large eyes, lipless mouths, and clawed hands and made a chirping noise. The aliens were looking into the house through the windows and were trying to get through the doors of the farmhouse.

When the police came by to investigate, all they found was an empty house with bullet holes in the windows and doors. A neighbor reported that the families left at 3:30 in the morning when they were attacked again by the same group of creatures.

Something had fallen from the sky that night and landed in the mountains. There was talk of a spaceship. Newspapers had a field day discussing flying saucers, gremlins and goblins.

Virginia Devil Monkey

In 1959, a beast sighting was reported in Saltville, Virginia where an aggressive creature charged a family's vehicle as they drove down a country road. The mysterious creature pursued their car for about a mile, digging deep scratches into their car door before disappearing. A few years later, two nurses were coming home from work and drove through the same area. The convertible top was ripped from their car by some dark beast that attacked them in the night. They were scared but not hurt.

A woman driving from Ohio was forced by some construction work to head down a dark county road not far from Roanoke, Virginia. It was 2:30 in the morning. As she drove into the night, a creature leaped in front of her car. It stood on its hind legs, six feet in the air. A cross between a large dog and a monkey-like creature, it was dark, hairy and had a long thin tail.

The Thunderbird (Ugalu) and the Tlanuwa (Great Mythic Hawk)

Are these creatures' stuff of myth and legend? Many of these huge birds are still being sighted.

Great birds of prey are found in many Indian legends. Two of the most distinct and infamous are the Thunderbird and the Cherokee Tlanuwa who are still being seen in both the Appalachians and the Ozark Mountains. Many people believe that these raptors are living fossils much like the prehistoric Pterodactyls. Both have a bad habit of swooping down and carrying off farm animals or small children.

Found on Native American totems, pottery and cave art, the thunderbird brings the power of the thunder and great storms along with the ability to shoot lightning from its eyes when it appears in the sky. The native peoples depict this creature as having a ten to twelve foot wingspan, with curling horns and teeth in its beak. In some stories, its head is featherless. Mount Katahdin in Maine is said to be the thunderbirds' home in the Appalachians. Native oral traditions also speak of medicine men with the ability to shapeshift into these winged predators.

The Tlanuwa, known also as "the copper birds", are thought to be giant mythological birds of prey that look much like a hawk. Reddish in color with impenetrable metal feathers and a six to eight foot wingspan, the Tlanuwa killed by striking victims with its sharp metal breast.

Raven Mocker

The Raven Mocker, or the Cherokee Kâ'lanû Ahkyeli'skï, steals the hearts from the sick and dying without leaving a mark on their skin. Eating the heart of its victim adds an extra year or more to its life. It is both a witch and an evil spirit that can appear as an elderly man, woman or transform itself into a wolf or raven with fiery wings who screeches in the darkness or even as a little girl. Though invisible when it is eating, a powerful medicine man can reveal its presence and chase it away from a dying victim until they are buried.

The Flatwoods or Frametown Monster

In 1952, Braxton County, in the Flatwoods of West Virginia, three young boys witnessed the downing of an object from the sky that crashed onto a local neighbor's farm. The boys then led adults to the area to investigate. There was a pungent smell as they walked through the woods.

One of the men used his flashlight to see what was going on when he noticed a red light nearby. He sighted a creature with a round, red looking face and a hooded cloak. The creature's eyes were a greenish-orange and the size of half dollars. It made a hissing sound. At ten feet tall and four foot wide, it seemed to be covered in a type of armor. Most witnesses seem to believe the creature to be armless. Others say it had small arms. When it glided towards them, they ran.

The Frametown Monster has a somewhat similar story. A couple was driving down a dark mountain road when their car stalled and refused to start. A bad smell filled the air, much like sulfur and rot. The couple paused and then stepped out of their car to see what was wrong with their vehicle. As they walked around their car, they spotted what they believed was a human with reptilian features, with claws on its hands and spindly legs. It disappeared into the woods. A few minutes later, their car was working again, and they left to report what they had witnessed.

It's All in Song

Musical instruments in Appalachia and the High-Lonesome

Instruments and Music Style

Mountain settlers originating from England, Ireland and Scotland influenced a majority of traditional American folk music. This sound later merged together with the tribal rhythms of blues and gospel. Birthed through the cultural pains of poverty and isolation, the Appalachian music style was strongly influenced by mountain stories and the people themselves.

Where many songs told a dark story, there were also songs of survival, faith and joy that became gospel in the lives of people living in the backwoods. Sung unaccompanied in a cappella or round-robin style, these songs were much like you would hear during a religious service.

Most people living in the mountains had little money and few musical instruments. Rhythmic sounds such as stomping, clapping, drumming, blowing into the tops of jugs or bottles, washboard, whistles or harmonica were common in social get-togethers when people sang or danced. Playing spoons became popular; their sound is much like castanets. A person playing spoons would hold two or more spoons by their handles in one hand and use another spoon in their other hand to strike in a sliding motion to make the sound.

Robert Young Antiques Collection - A Unique Collection of Five Mountain Banjos c.1888-1920 from Virginia and North Carolina

Over time, other types of instruments joined the mix. Around the 1740s, a fiddler from Scotland named Neil Gow developed the short bow - saw stroke technique in fiddle playing that is the foundation of the Appalachian fiddle style.

In the mid-1800s, slaves who escaped into the mountains and eventually settled there introduced a major musical instrument to the Appalachians. Called an akonting, it was first created in Arabia, coming to Africa through Arab conquest. This instrument had a skin-headed gourd body, two long melody strings, and one short drone string and became very popular in the United States. This instrument was a major prototype of the modern day banjo.

Another instrument developed in Africa was the washtub bass. The washtub bass or gutbucket is an instrument that uses a metal washtub, a length of gut or wire and a stick or staff. Using the washtub as a resonator, the gut or wire is connected to the washtub in the center. The other end of the gut or wire is connected to the top of the stick or staff. This piece stands tight against the outside rim of the washtub. The tub is held down by the player's foot sitting on top of it. The stick or staff is creating stress by pulling the gut or wire forward or backward. When strummed, the stress creates different tones. The tighter the string, the higher the tone.

Washtub bass;
US National Archives and Records Adminstration photo

Other instruments were introduced to create the mountain sound that came from a truly different age. The jews or jaws harp has been around since the medieval period and were used throughout Europe. Its "twang" sound is very popular in Old Time music.

Another instrument that was popular was the psaltery. A psaltery is a small hand-held harp that can be played upright or played flat on your lap. It has the zither "zing" and its history goes back to biblical times.

In Kentucky in 1880, a zither-like instrument called a mountain dulcimer was being built in the Appalachians for sale. It was different from the hammered dulcimer, in that instead of being struck by mallets, it was plucked with the fingers. With the revival of folk music in America in the 1950s through the 1970s, the popularity of this instrument has soared.

By 1910, the "three dollar guitar" became a popular mail-order instrument in America as well as the lute-like mandolin. Stores began to open to sell all types of musical instruments and as time went on, the art of high-quality musical instrument making became a popular craft in the Appalachians.

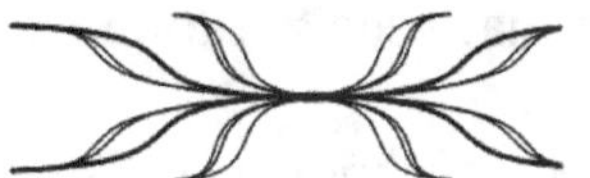

Ballard Branch Bogtrotters Band,
Galax, Va. 1934-1942
- US National Archives and Records Administration

The musical ethnic-blend, which became traditional American music, was also coined "old time" in 1923. A branch of this style that used predominately banjo, guitar and mandolin was for dance music. In 1945, that branch became known as Bluegrass after singer and songwriter Bill Monroe's musical group, *The Blue Grass Boys*. Commercial recordings began to be popular and people flooded to remote mountain areas to collect songs and music pieces. Rural mountain people began to feel outsiders were beginning to take away what traditional value they had left, and kept many of their works inside their personal community.

The third transition of traditional American music occurred in the 1920s and became known as "country" music. Steel guitar and a developed high-pitched singing style called, the "high-lonesome" sound, made a permanent mark in American music history. The original wail-like style was created and recorded by an Appalachian old-time singer from Daisy, Kentucky. His name was Roscoe Holcomb (1918-1981) and his sound influenced many in the country field.

Roscoe Holcomb US National Archives and Records Administration

A singer and musician, Roscoe Holcomb was a well-known figure in the Appalachian folk music scene. Some of Holcomb's best work was sung a cappella in the Old Regular Baptist tradition. It was his friend John Cohen who coined the expression, "High-lonesome sound," for which Holcomb became famous. He also played four instruments: Guitar, banjo, harmonica, and fiddle.

Holcomb spent a great deal of his life working in the coalmines of Kentucky. He suffered from asthma and emphysema as a result. Holcomb died in a nursing home at the age of 68 in 1981.

A lot of mountain history was handed-down by way of poems, songs, stories and sayings. Those that were able to write, recorded them in ledgers and diaries. Those less 'school-educated' used the power of their own voice. In the mountains, the telling of stories was how most things were remembered.

Haint*or Haint Not (A Story)

**** **Haint** (hānt) n. Southern expression for a spirit who haunts.

'Thanks for the tobacco and the new pipe. I'm in sore need of it. Now I can take my old one apart and clean it. Have you had a chance to look around the mountainside and talk to any folks?"

Seeing the look of frustration on my face, the old woman laughed.

"You might have to have the local pastor introduce you this Sunday during service. Most people won't talk to you before you do. Heard you were gathering information on the healing folk in this area, so I'm guessing that is why you came to see me?"

She turned and opened her oven door. Pulling out the iron skillet from the heat, the fragrant smell of fresh corn bread filled her kitchen as I sat at her table. Coffee was percolating on the top of the stove.

"Are you here today for some recipes for healings and workings, or are you here for a reckoning?"

Explaining that I was planning to stay in the area for the next couple of weeks to gather information for my book, Granny Buck said she could take me out to the hillside with her tomorrow if I could to meet her on her porch at 5:30 in the morning. Having settled the time for our next meeting, she gazed thoughtfully out the window for a moment. Slowly shaking her head, she answered her own question:

"A reckoning, then."

Seeing that I didn't know exactly what she meant, she explained that there were many kinds of reckonings. Some reckonings were of biblical proportions (like the pastor says). and some everyday-like for people like you and me. A reckoning could mean that a person needs to come to an understanding of what is going on around them. A lot of times, they don't see. Sometimes, the only way these people can understand a reckoning is to tell a story that applies to it. So, if I was willing, she wanted to tell me a story after we ate.

Cutting the corn bread, she took a small piece and threw it out the window.

"For the critters living outside," was her explanation. She then placed a warm piece of bread and a chunk of butter on a plate and handed it to me. A hot cup of coffee was placed by my side on the table. We ate in silence.

After the meal, we sat in the kitchen by the fireplace. The old woman stoked up the fire and sat back in her chair. Smiling at me sitting across from her, she packed some tobacco in her pipe and lit it. Staring into the fire, she began her tale:

"A little over forty years ago, the area around here was mostly rocks and wood. Families had their homesteads scattered across the mountain valleys, and the only people who ever saw them on a regular basis was the migrant farm workers passing through, the cunning folk out looking for herbs and such, and the mailman who drove up from Piney Ridge Post Office to deliver mail.

People around here were always lookin' for a bit of news they could share and talk about. This was no different than on that April morning that Marvin Lamb was found dead. Lemmie Kane, the mailman, found him all twisted in the powdered dirt and gray in the face. His head was dipped down into the darkness of the rain trench that was on the side of the house. It had rained real hard the day before, and he must have fallen in the rain and didn't get back up. Heart attack, he guessed.

Seein' as how the doctor wouldn't be driving into the area to check on things for at least another week, Lemmie went inside Lamb's cabin and took the quilt off the bed to cover him up with. Then he drove two miles up the road to Plate's farm to get a truck and a hand to take old Marvin Lamb down to Mock's Funeral Home in town.

The town of Rowenwood at that time consisted of a dry goods/grocery and feed store, an old gas station, a café, a bakery, the community church and Mock's Funeral Home. Albert Mock was proud of the service he gave his small community and considered himself to be one of the few educated people in town.

Looking down at Marvin Lamb's body on the table, Albert had to agree with the postman. Yep; heart attack. No need to put him in cold storage until Doc came. Lamb didn't have family around here to pay the bill, but he figured the church community would raise enough money to have him buried in the local cemetery. Rolling up his sleeves, Albert Mock covered the body back up and thanked the postman. He needed to get it washed and ready to be laid out.

Three days later, old Marvin was in the ground. A couple of the ladies from the Church of Our Savior drove over to his home place to pack up his stuff and see if he had any addresses of family that there in his papers. He had kept to himself after his wife died. He even stopped going to church and wouldn't have anything to do with the people there. Some of his neighbors hadn't seen him in years. Lemmie used to tell stories of coming up to deliver mail and finding Marvin mumbling to himself and walking in circles around in the woods behind his house...."

The old woman stopped speaking and relit her pipe. As she puffed, the smoke from it spiraled into the air and disappeared. She gazed up towards the ceiling for a minute or so, then quietly said, "You might need to know who the characters are in this story; there's a few. Let's see; I'll start with Silas…

I

"Old Silas Mabey was the local bone picker. For years, he sold or traded to his neighbors many of the bones he found for their workings or charms. His Mam and grandpa had taught him what to look for in the woods and hillsides, and how to clean them up. His family had a strong Powwow/healer bloodline, and though Silas was a bit slow, they taught him the family ways.

It was said that many of the animal bones he sold to people in the past few months had a funny smell to them. Folks joked that it was because Silas carried his bones as well as pieces of dead animals in his coat pockets and didn't clean them out at the end of the day. He had that dirty old coat for a lot of years. Probably slept in it, too.

In those past few months, Silas had gotten to where he restocked a lot of the bones from the dead animals he found behind Marvin Lamb's old place. Silas found more carcasses there than most of the places he looked. Some of the dead things still had hunks of meat on their bones. Right queer, it was. The meat would be splotched bright red and greasy brown in color. It was almost as if the flesh didn't know if it was still alive or dead. Old Silas would later tell people that he would have normally saved most meat he found for himself to eat later, but not that mess. He wasn't going to put that in his mouth for nothing. No Sir.

Silas Mabey had noticed the bare circle on old Marvin's land had gotten larger over the past few months; lots of bones and dead grass around it. There were even a few trees that looked like the life was just sucked from them. He later told people, he guessed the talk was true…"

The old woman got up to stir the fire. Returning to her chair, she took a crocheted throw from the back of it and wrapped it around her. She continued:

"Word was that a conjure woman by the name of Grannie Pickler was said to have cursed old Marvin because of the hateful things he said to her about her grandson Riley.

Riley had died in a coal mine cave-in. He was only fourteen. No Sir; talking ill of the dead just gets you noticed by haints. It sure was strange the way Marvin died. They thought it was heart attack, but word was he had sucked a lot of dust up in his lungs. Looked to me like the curse, just like chickens, had come home to roost."

The old woman paused and looked at the writer in the chair across from her. The young man was intensely scribbling down notes and looked up when she stopped. Taking a sip of her coffee, she asked,

"How much do you know about conjure magic? Anything? That's okay; no need to speak. I'll just tell you, it's powerful stuff, and Alma Pickler at that time was known to be strong with it. Anyway, so…

Sukie Collins lived with her husband and his family a mile or so from here. She recalled that when she was twelve years old, her Mam told her to meet the other churchwomen at Lamb's cabin to help clean. It was the neighborly thing to do. They had heard from the pastor that some relatives of the dead man had been found and wanted to come and look at the property before making any decisions about it".

This is what she told all of us later that same week:

"I was cutting through the woods when I saw Granny Pickler. I didn't want her to notice me, so I stopped by a tree and watched her a bit…

Alma Pickler had been watching at the rim of the woods as the women from town cleaned out Marvin Lamb's cabin. Slipping her hand into her pocket, she pulled the small stick figure out. A tear rolled down her cheek as she talked to it.

"I told him he would know how my Riley had felt; in darkness, unable to breathe and fighting for his life. I guess he knows now." Untying the red string, the sticks and rags came apart as she placed them in the hole she had dug with a spoon.

"Back to the earth with you," she said.

She pushed the soil over top of it with her boot. No one noticed her but Sukie as she walked away into the trees."

Granny Buck got up and threw another log on the fire. "Now; the new family that moved into Martin Lamb's old cabin didn't really know him either. His great nephew Sam Carlson ended up with the house and land. He, his wife Susan Ann and a cousin of his came up the mountain to see what Sam had now owned. They were a young family, just starting out and didn't have much, and though Sam was sad his great-uncle had died, he was glad for the windfall. They, along with Sam's cousin Joseph, decided to move to the area in early September, 1957…"

II

"Wow, it's like coming to a whole new country or something, Susan Ann couldn't help but think. Looks different, feels different; it even smells different". She let go of her breathe as her nose wrinkled. "A dry smell and cow manure, oh boy".

The girl went out to the gravel road by the house and took a box out of her husband's truck.

"At least there's plenty to do. Lots of unpacking. Meeting the pastor of the local church when we first came up to look at the property, made a difference. He's been really helpful. Especially about our 'neighbors' if you call them that. Nearest one two miles away. New people settling in the area will bring the curious by, I bet. It won't be too long before Sam and Susan Ann Carlson and Joseph McCory will fit right into the community".

She wondered if she was going to miss their apartment in Stoneville. There's a big difference between living in a city not far from the coast, to moving and living in semi-seclusion on a mountain hillside. John Madison County is on the other side of the state from where they lived. Sure is pretty, though; wild looking, too.

"We got all the boxes in the right rooms, Susan Ann. Let's see if we can get that old stove working and put some coffee on." Wiping his face, Sam smiled as he looked up at her. "Joey's still upstairs putting the beds together."

"I am so glad you boys like to work real hard. It sure was a mess getting everything here. Your other cousins helping us out made a real difference. We were able to get it done in three days; now, it might take three years to unpack." With a tired smile, Susan pulled a kitchen chair back and sat down. "My legs are numb. It sure has been a long couple of days."

264

After a hot dinner, Susan Ann, Sam and Joe discussed their upcoming week. The guys hoped she wouldn't get too bored as they had to go into the city fifteen miles away to work. Both had new jobs and were curious as to how their first day would be. Laughing, Susan Ann reassured them she had plenty to do, unpacking and cleaning. "Besides", she said, "someone has to cook dinner when they bring their butts home from work." Joe let out a snort and Sam grinned. Exhausted, they rose from the table and went to bed.

The morning came early, and arm and arm, Susan and Sam walked to Sam's truck. Joey was half asleep in the passenger seat already.

"We'll be home around six. All of us have something new to do today. Should make for good dinner conversation." Sam hugged his wife.

"Don't do any heavy lifting. Just unbox the small stuff today. Joe and I will help unpack some when we get home. We've got Sunday off. That's probably going to be the best time to set up your loom in the back shed". Joe checked the roof, and it seemed to be in decent shape. Sam bent down towards her and kissed her cheek. "Love ya."

She waved at them as the truck torn off down the gravel road.

By late afternoon, Susan Ann took a break. She had already unpacked maybe a dozen boxes, washed and put up all the plates and glasses, and made a pitcher of iced tea. She eyed the bag of lemon drop cookies she had bought from the bakery in town the day before. Pouring a glass of cold tea, she grabbed the bag and went to sit on the front porch.

III

Susan Ann stretched back in her front porch chair and watched the sun climb between the trees from where she was sitting. The land she saw around her was flush with springtime. Wildflowers and green things attracted the birds and animals around her front yard and down through the mountain area below. Quite a difference between the front acreage and the back lot where Sam's great-uncle had his outbuildings. The backyard was grassy and had an apple tree by the back door. About two hundred yards further out, the back property changed dramatically; many of the animal pens, a storage building and the chicken coop were old and crumbling and needed to be rebuilt. The weaving shed (as she called it) seemed to be in pretty good shape and was built closer to the house. It could've used a coat of paint though. The footpaths leading to anywhere were dirt. She noticed that if a good wind came through, the air around the pens blew the dry earth from the ground, giving the sky around them a dirty brown look. She was thinking of asking Sam, to put some gravel down in the back pathways to keep the stuff from being tracked into the house. As she was making these plans, Susan Ann's first visitor came out of the trees in front of her and crossed the gravel road.

As the man approached, Susan Ann could help but grin at the sight. He seemed to be around six foot tall and thin. His face was the face of a younger man's, though she thought he was probably in his late 50s.

Her unusual visitor was dressed in a mix-matched coloring of clothing that was covered with a greasy looking, long gray coat. The pair of old Army boots on his feet had seen better days. His gray-streaked, long hair was tied back, and an old brown felt hat kind of sat on his head. His pockets seemed to be filled to bursting with things and slung over his shoulder was a birch bark box with a strap and a fur pouch. Spotting her, he grinned and waved.

Approaching the front porch, he tipped his hat and said, "I heered you folks was moving into Marvin's old place. Came to introduce myself. Name's Silas. Silas Mabey. We're neighbors. My family's farm is about six miles west of here at Crescent Crown. Just came to welcome ya'll and see if you need anything. "Round here, I bring things to people that need things."

Grinning, Susan Ann stood and looked at him for a few moments. Then, waving him up the steps, she invited him to sit on the porch. Thanking her, he shuffled up onto the porch to the chair.

As he was getting comfortable, the girl went back inside and into the kitchen to pour him a glass of tea and get a plate to put cookies on. She handed him the glass and plate. He put the glass on the porch by the chair, and reaching for a cookie, he said:

"Mighty kind. Here's hoping the blessings of the day will visit your door."

They sat together in silence until the cookies were eaten. The girl then asked Silas about the area her family had just moved into. He pushed his hat back, leaned back into the chair and talked. An hour later and Susan Ann didn't know where the time went. As he talked, the young woman began to realize that Silas was a little mentally slow but understood most things. He seemed gentle enough.

He talked about his family. He said he came from a lengthy line of Powwow healers and Grannie women, and even though he was "half a mind", he was taught the ways through his mother and his grandfather. He learned the signs, natural ways of healing, as well as the Bible quotes to draw fire or to stop bleeding.

He also had some delightful stories about her neighbors. They set her off in a fit of giggles. When he found out Susan Ann was a weaver, Silas told her about Millie and Jessie Morland. They lived about eight miles away by Bear Creek. They were potters who dug their own clay and built their own fire pit for firing and glazing the pottery they made. They sold, or sometimes barter, their wares in town.

He mentioned the Pastor and his church. It was the only church that was built around the area. Social gatherings such as births, weddings and burials were when you saw folk. He said the latest church burial was three months ago. Clarke Jessim was his name. He had a small patch of land north of here. Besides a bit of farming, he kept bees. Silas glanced up at her from his chair, saw she was listening and began his tale.

"Old Clarke Jessim used to tell his bees everything. He trusted them more than people and would spend hours talking to them as he tended their hives. About three months ago, the elderly beekeeper collapsed at the seed store while getting some groceries and died.

On the day when the old man was to be buried, a great swarm of bees gathered around the top of the door of the church while the preacher was conducting the funeral. The people that came to pay their respects had to leave by the side door. Why, some of those bees even landed on Jessim's white shirt he was being buried in and wouldn't leave! A couple of weeks after Old Clarke was in the ground, his cousin, Abram, finally took the boxes over to his farm. By then, most of the bees had left.

Commons

We sat in silence as he finished his tale. The ice clinking in our glasses as we finished our tea. Then, rising from his chair, he looked over at me and started going through his pockets. Smiling, he found what he was looking for.

In the dirty paper bag, the old man had pulled out eight reddish knots of heartwood pine. He called them "lighter knots." Chuckling, he explained that if we needed a fire started really fast, we should put a piece of this in the firewood along with some paper or twigs. "It's the sap in it that catches fire real quick and burns hot," he said. He called it, "a neighbor-welcome present." This, "and a few other things" is what he sold to the people that lived in the area.

Thanking me for my time, he lumbered off the porch and walked towards the woods. Raising his hat from his head with a, "See ya soon," he disappeared through the trees.

IV

Within the next few weeks, summer quickly disappeared, and we settled down into the beginnings of fall. The household things were finally unpacked, and Susan Ann's loom had been set up in the side building. She usually went there after she got the guys off to work.

Sam and Joe had already fallen into a routine: up early in the morning, grabbing a packed lunch made the night before, and disappearing out the front door to the truck. The ride to work was 45 minutes long, so they had to time it out to clock in for their shifts. Susan Ann seldom saw them coming home before dark when they were working.

They all tried though, to go to Sunday service at the church. They wanted to meet the families that were considered their neighbors, though homesteads were sometimes miles apart. Church of Our Savior was the only church on this side of the mountain. The church, and the meeting hall downtown, is where all the people gathered and socialized. The only other church around, Founder's Grace Methodist Church, was in Compton Valley, nine miles away.

Susan Ann, Sam and Joe met several folks that lived in the area at these gatherings. One was an older farming couple, named Bramie and Jean Plate. Jean had baked a pie for their new neighbors the week before. They had all thanked her and said it was delicious. Smiling, she said,

"My Mam used to say, 'a word of praise is equal to ointment on a sore.'"

The old farmwife wiped her hands with her handkerchief. Looking up into Susan Ann's face, she softly spoke:

"A tree is known by its fruit, not by the leaves it bears. Did any of your family ever live around here?"

269

"I don't think so. My family name is Darby. Most of that line came from Illinois."

"You remind me of somebody…" Jean then glanced across the back of the room at the milling people.

"Bramie, there's Pastor Page. I need to talk to him about the Sunday school."

Taking her husband's arm, Bramie and Jean smiled and waved as they walked away and toward the Minister.

Susan Ann recognized the Morland's names when she was introduced to them after service, and really liked Millie and her husband. Short and small, with bright red hair, Millie Morland's smile lit up a room, and she talked a mile a minute. Her husband Jessie's dark eyes would look over at her, and he'd quietly smile as she jumped from one subject to another.

Millie invited Susan Ann, Sam and Joe up to their place for a kiln firing party in September. She was happy to know that Susan Ann was a weaver and used hand-dyed skeins for her weaving. Susan Ann liked the fact that Millie liked to experiment and mixed natural dyes into her glazes for her pottery. They talked about wild plants and the color dyes produced from them.

The next morning, Susan Ann walked down the dusty path to the shed to work on her loom. She had created a pattern on paper a few days before to weave. Susan Ann loved bright colors. She had already dyed two batches of yarn, a soft indigo blue and a lemon yellow. There were traces of dye on her hands, especially her finger tips. She didn't mind, as both batches of color produced a good color on the yarn and thread. The colors brought some life into

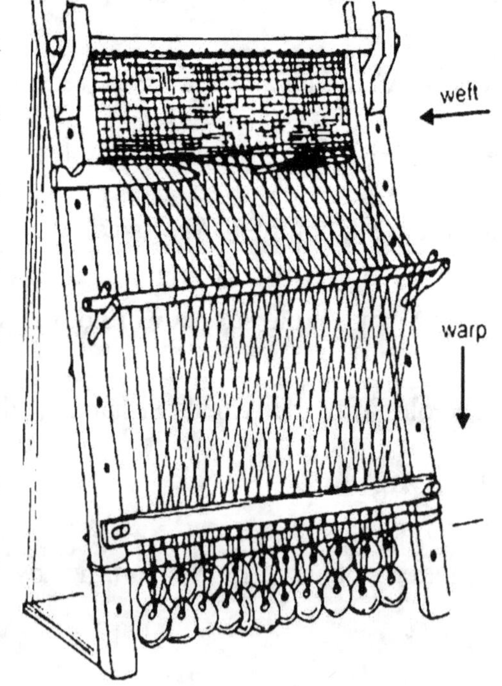

270

the gray looking shed. She pulled a russet brown and crimson spool from the workroom's cabinet to add to the mix. She then measured out the warp threads according to color and tied them to the back roller of the loom and threaded them through. Sam had attached long warps, instead of short, to the loom to reduce the number of times she had to rethread the same project. The only drawback was she couldn't take the unfinished product off the loom. She needed to cover it at night.

The hours rushed by as her fingers slid across the shuttle, and her hands and loom blended the colors to create the bright cloth. Looking up at the western setting sun, she was amazed at how fast time flew. She needed to finish what she was doing and wash up, so she could get dinner.

Sam had called the local quarry while he was on break at work the day before, and they were having someone coming by around about three o'clock tomorrow to dump a truck full of gravel. Hopefully, this Sunday after church, Sam and Joe can paint the outside of the building they had set up the loom in. It was the only solid building in the back; the other two and the chicken coop were all crumbly and caved in.   When they first moved in and Susan Ann told the boys her plans, Joe had teased her about the outside property where the only good building sat. He looked at the roughly circular sixty feet of dusty, dry, dead bushes and trees around the outbuildings, and told her that the only living thing out there moving around would be Susan Ann working on her loom! Thank goodness the front piece of land was green, and the rest of the forest was alive. Laughing, Susan Ann said it was nothing a little rain and some gravel in the pathways wouldn't cure, and they all went in the house to have dinner.

Luke and Mike were the men that brought the gravel by that afternoon. Mike was the older and burlier one of the two. He was the dump truck driver. Luke was skinnier and younger. His brown hair was shaved close to his scalp, and his ears stuck out on both sides of his head. They both wore gray work pants and matching shirts with a name patch on them.

As they drove up, Mike asked Susan Ann where she wanted the gravel. She explained she wanted to cover the dirt paths behind the house to keep the dust down and told them to drive into the back by the old chicken coop.

When the men got out, the one called Luke looked blankly out onto the barren field. His face seemed to drain of color. Turning to look at Susan Ann he said:

"It doesn't seem right back here. Lots of dead stuff and it feels bad. Are you working out there by yourself?" Before she could answer, he mumbled, "I can see why your neighbors think old Marvin's haint is still walking around."

Susan Ann thought she had gotten used to mountain bluntness, but this man was an asshole. Stepping back from the man as he spoke, the angry voice inside her head shouted, "What was he trying to do, scare me?"

Her voice went from friendly to chilly; she almost wanted to order the men off her property.

Mike saw the situation, stared and frowned at Luke. Luke made a face at him and said:

"What? They say he be walkin' round in circles looking for something…"

"Shut up, Luke. That's crazy talkin'."

Mike tried to smooth it over for Susan Ann.

"Well, you know how stories are Miz Carlson… a lot of people around here believe haints and weird things can be found in the mountains. Luke's just spoofin."

Grabbing the skinny man by his shoulders, Mike pushed Luke back into the truck. Getting in himself, Mike backed the vehicle up and poured the gravel into a pile by the pathway. He then gave Susan Ann a shovel and a rake and told her he would come by in the next week or so and pick them up after the work was done. Sam had already paid for the delivery.

V

Weeks passed. With steady jobs and a couple of sales from Susan Ann's weavings, the little family seemed content. The young woman tried to work about three to five hours a day either on her loom or setting up dye batches for her weaving material. While the boys were in town working, she was also able to put the gravel down on the paths, and some of the dusk settled. She thought by fall it would be looking good. Also, Sam and Joe were making plans to rebuild some of the back buildings.

The September sun brought on hot, muggy, dog days. Susan Ann would go down to the back building around seven-thirty in the morning, while the air was still cool. The girl ignored the bleakness of the area behind her as she worked, but there were times when she was out there that she just didn't feel right. She jokingly thought she should have been a tough farm girl by now, but sometimes when she was out back on her loom, she felt physically weak, and her head would swim. There were moments when it was hard for her to remember anything. It only lasted a second or two, and then it would ease off. Her skin would feel itchy sometimes, too. She wasn't sleeping too well either; weird dreams. She was thinking maybe the heat, or the tree pollen were getting to her, and that if it continued in the next week or so, she may have to go into town to see the doctor. He should be coming back through soon. There was no need to say anything to Sam right then.

That morning, Susan Ann went out to check the dye buckets. She had placed them by the apple tree, and when looking in, she was happy with the results. One bucket was going to produce a beautiful wine-red color yarn, the other a Kelley green. When dying the skeins used for her loom, she tried to keep her gloves on, but seeing the fresh color on the yarn and thread would result in her being eventually bare-handed when she rinsed the materials. The results were that her hands almost constantly, had patches of dye on them. Except for a blue tinge, the natural colors easily faded. They joked about it at church saying Susan Ann just wanted to bring more color into everyone's lives.

Later that evening, the laughter around the table after dinner just completed a perfect day for them all. A cool breeze had come in during the early evening, and by dark the family was ready for bed. Saying goodnight to Joe, Susan Ann and Sam went to their room. Sam fell asleep as soon as his head touched the pillow. Restless, Susan Ann got up and rinsed her face and hands in the bathroom sink.

Returning to the room, she sat back down on her side of the bed and looked out the back window. The full moon's light bathed the back-property area, giving the circle of ground a kind of silvery look. The stripped trees and the dried-up bushes gleamed. "Wait a minute…is something moving back there?" A fiery ball appeared, and there was a shadowy movement in the ghostly trees.

Susan Ann watched as the light seemed to bounce and move. Leaving the room, she went down the steps and opened the back door. All she saw was trees, bushes and dead ground when she was looking out. It was too quiet back there in the darkness. It gave her a shiver. Perhaps it was a light reflection from a truck coming up the mountain. She was just letting stupid things worry her. She shut the door and went up to bed.

The next morning, Susan Ann went to uncover her loom. She noticed something not far from her on the dirt path. It was a dead opossum. It was lying on its back with its mouth open. It had a funny blue tinge to it. "Oh no", she thought. She hoped the pitiful thing didn't get into any of her dye buckets. Further up the path, she noticed a dead robin lying in the dust by one of the dried-up trees. It looked like it had gotten sick before it died, and brought up its last meal. Its beak was open, and its feet blue and drawn up as well. She checked the buckets and was confused. Nope, nothing had gotten into the buckets. Instead of working on the loom, Susan Ann went back into the house and waited for the boys to come home.

Both fellows listened as she told her tale, starting with the men who had brought the gravel the week before. The boys teased her about old Marvin's haint coming to visit and said she should stay on the living end of the property. She spoke to them about the flickering light and the shadowy movement in the woods. After some discussion, they concluded it was something that the mountain people call a Will-o-wisp, perhaps some natural gas coming up through the soil. Together, they all went out back and walked through the circle of trees. The whole area looked washed out.

Sam had been meaning to contact the county agent about the property, but he knew that before they moved there, there was a drought and patches of mountainside had dried up. He was noticing, too, that the well water was starting to taste kind of sour. Frowning, he thought about what he heard at the mill, and said to himself, "We are not living on cursed land". Yeah, he had heard the town gossip about how his uncle died: "Yes, it sure was strange, and the way the property looks in the back would scare anybody. The old mailman doesn't help either. Comes around here looking for any tidbit of gossip he can pass on to the other neighbors. Can't believe anyone would allow himself to be called, 'Lemmie,' and the old man keeps telling the story of finding my uncle on the property to anyone who will listen".

Glancing over at his wife, Sam noticed Susan Ann wasn't looking so hot either; she looked kind of faded. "Maybe she needs to get off the property more", he thought. She certainly wasn't sleeping and was restless. He decided he would have to look into it soon. The meal ended. They all cleaned up the room afterwards. Then, saying good-night to Joey, they went up to their room.

Hours later, Susan Ann rose up from her bed and screamed into the night, "No, help her! She's bleeding! Hurry! She's going to die!" Sam held her as she woke up from her nightmare.

VI

Dressed for work, Sam stood next to her in the driveway and asked her not to go out to the back building to her loom while they were gone. After all that had happened, he felt she needed rest. He reached over and brushed his hand across her pale face. Then, bending down to kiss her, he opened his truck door and got in to leave. Joe waved from the other side of the seat. "Call us if you need us, Susan Ann. One, if not both of us will be back here quick as a flash!" Waving and beeping the horn, they backed out and started down the road.

Around ten that morning, Silas came through the woods and approached her on the porch. He said he had heard her cries in the night and hoped she was feeling better. Smiling, he handed her a plastic grocery bag filled with Indian paintbrush flowers he had picked. She loved the flowers but wondered how he had heard her. "Was Silas roaming in the woods around the house in the dark?"

Thanking him as he sat down in the chair next to her on the porch, she explained that she had had a bad nightmare. He asked her to tell him. If nothing else, he said, she might feel better talking it out. Susan Ann began:

"In the dream, it was raining. I saw a young girl, maybe thirteen years old, pick up the axe from the porch of her house and head for a small woodshed, her head hanging down and her mouth was in a tight line. A voice hollered out from inside the house she was leaving saying, 'No more sass, Mary Agnes! I asked you to get kindling two hours ago. Your Mam should be back soon from her meeting. Get it done."

I see her as she goes into the woodshed. Placing branches on a log chopping block, the girl began to swing the axe and mutter as she worked. The more she chopped, the more agitated she seemed, slinging the smaller pieces of wood to the floor. Not paying attention to what she was doing, the axe went down on to her leg. There was so much blood! She looked so scared. She started to fall...then I woke up screaming. I never felt so helpless. There was nothing I could do. It was so real..."

Silas patted her hand as she stared off.

"Perhaps you can help, Susan Ann. Did you know the girl? What did the house look like? It hasn't rained around here for a while, so maybe something will happen when it does."

Shaking her head, she smiled at Silas and said, "Okay, I'll tell you. I know you believe in that kind of stuff, and I don't want to hurt your feelings, but it was probably just a dream."

She stepped inside to her kitchen to get him some tea. Handing him a glass, she continued:

"I haven't been sleeping well recently. Headaches. Sometimes I wake up gasping for air like I forget to breathe. The gasping thing has only happened twice, and Sam only knows about one time. Food is starting to make me sick, too. Heck, for all I know, I might even be seeing things. I'm trying to bide my time; I've got another appointment with the doctor in Rowenwood. If it gets any worse, Sam said he was taking me over to the county hospital."

It finally rained ten days later. The plants and the animals outside sure did like it. It had been hot and dry for a while. Susan Ann looked out her living-room window at the grayness in the mountains and trees. It will soon be three o'clock. Well, so far so good. Silas promised he would come by if he heard anything. Meanwhile, she needed to rest.

That same day, on the other side of the mountain, not far from HWY 64, Mary Agnes came out of her family's house pouting and angry. Her family's home was a neat gray and blue trimmed farmhouse, stoutly built, that had seen many generations of the McFee family being born, growing up or dying.

The heavy rain falling around her, soured her mood even more. She walked over to the tool shed and saw the axe lying on the shed's porch. Grabbing the handle of the axe, she dragged the back of the head of it across the wood porch of the building. It made a satisfying, loud, scratchy noise. It almost made her feel better.

She ran up the steps next door and into the woodshed. Grabbing some of the smaller pieces of wood from the pile, she placed them on the chopping block. She swung the ax haphazardly as she worked, slinging the pieces to the floor. Because she was irritated, she wasn't paying attention when it happened.

Uuh! The axe seemed to bounce off her leg, and then it fell to the ground. The girl looked down, confused. She didn't seem to react at all. Then, with the burning numbness and the warm red fluid running down her leg, she knew she was in trouble. She hollered for help, but she doubted her father could hear from the house. Her shouts were deadened by the rain outside. She stood, looking down at herself, then sliding into shock, she fell onto the earthen floor.

A moment later, the woodshed door opened, and Silas looked down at the girl prone on the shed floor. Slapping his hand on the side of his jeans, he thought: "I knew it! Knew it! Knew it! Knew it! Won't Miz Carlson be surprised?!"

Quickly moving over to her, he cut a small portion of her pant leg, so he could see the wound. It had missed the artery. Silas took his belt off and applied a tourniquet to her leg. For a couple of minutes, he sat with her semi-conscious form waiting for the blood to slow. Then, he picked up the young girl and hurried her to the house, shouting as he went. Her father opened the door, helped them inside, and got the first aid kit.

After talking to Susan Ann about the house and the girl's appearance in her dream, he had a few days to figure out who he thought it was and waited in the rain at their farm to see if he could help her if she accidently cut herself. He told her father; Susan Ann Carlson saw it in a nightmare and told him. The word spread.

On Sunday, after church, Susan Ann was approached by members of the congregation, including Mary Agnes and her father, who brought her a ham and a dozen fresh eggs. After hearing about the story that Silas had told Mr. McFee when they were wrapping Mary Agnes's leg, they all believed Susan Ann had the sight, and the nightmare was a warning.

Embarrassed, she told them is was probably a coincidence; it had never happened to her before and she hasn't been feeling well. Though Sam stood by her, he seemed agitated and ready to leave. Joe walked up to Sam's side and asked when they were going. He had noticed Susan Ann's church friends were watching her silently.

Two days later, it all came to a head. Susan Ann was feeling poorly and stayed in bed after the boys went to work. Sam almost didn't go. He had looked down at his wife, saw the grayness in her face and realized how thin she looked. In less than five weeks, he could hardly recognize her from the robust girl who came to their new home. It was only because she pushed him out the door that he went to the mill that day.

Lying in their bed, Susan Ann kept hearing the phone ringing, but she just didn't feel up to going downstairs to answer it. About thirty minutes later, she heard a knock on the door. Her mind had been in a fog all morning. She heard the knock three times before she before she could drag herself downstairs to answer it.

Opening her door, she saw a heavy-set man in his early fifties looking down at her on the porch. His boots, jeans and jacket all looked dusty. Taking off his cap, he said,

"Miz Carlson? I know you don't know me, but my name is Jeremy Klute."

Dazed, she continued to stare out the door as if he hadn't said a word.

"Miz Carlson, are you okay?"

She looked at him and started to speak, "I…"

He caught her as she fell forward in a heap. Picking up her slight form, the man carried her off the porch. As they were going down the steps and into the yard, she noticed a car quickly coming down the road. A light flashed on top of the hood.

From that point, everything became a haze for her. The man gently laid her down on the grass and looked up as the sheriff and the doctor approached quickly from the car. Popping his bag open, the doctor removed a stethoscope. She felt the coldness on her chest as he checked her heart rate. He then felt her face, rubbed her hands and called her name until she replied. When he thought she was stabilized, the doctor asked the man to pick her up again and lay her in the back of the sheriff's car. The man confirmed to the sheriff that he would shut her house up and meet them in a few minutes. The sheriff had folded his jacket and placed it under her head. As the car turned around in the driveway, the doctor looked at her in the back seat and said,

"Miz Carlson, the sheriff and I are taking you over to the county hospital. Your husband and his cousin have been informed, and will meet you there for sign in. Hold on, we might be going a little fast."

A few days later, Susan Ann woke up in a brightly lit room in the hospital. Sam was asleep in a recliner next to her and Joey was just coming through the door with two cups of coffee. Sitting the coffee on the side table, Joey approached.

"You sure did scare us, Susan Ann," Smiling, the young man gave her shoulder a little squeeze.

Hearing his cousin talking, Sam opened his eyes, stretched and sat up in the chair.

Walking over and planting a kiss on his wife's cheek, his eyes looked thoughtful.

"Hey, Darling'. Feeling better?"

"Hey yourself. What's going on? Is everything okay?"

"Is now, but if I had known what was going on with that property, we would have never moved there. You almost died. If we keep living there, we might have all died."

"You're scaring me. What's going on?!"

The door opened, and a nurse came into the room with her breakfast tray. Setting it down, she looked over at the boys and said,

"I need for you to step out a moment, so the doctor can check on her. You can come back in while she is eating breakfast."

Giving her a hug, Sam said, "Look, Susan Ann, don't worry about it. You're okay now. Joey and I are going to go downstairs for a few minutes. Relax and eat your breakfast. We'll be back in a little bit, and then maybe we can help explain it to you." He bent down and kissed her, and then they left the room.

When the boys returned to the room a half an hour later, Susan Ann was visibly upset.

"Methane poisoning? Sam, the doctor said I had methane poisoning! How on earth did that happen?"

"Calm down, sweetheart. It was a shock to us as much as it was to you. I guess we weren't prepared to live here. Anyway, most people, even in the mountains, would not have recognized it unless they grew up in a coal mining town. Even then, what happened on our property was a rare occurrence.

While Joey and I were down stairs, we ran into someone who was coming to see you. He should be up in a minute. I think you might want to hear what he has to say."

There was a tapping on Susan Ann's door. Joey opened it to reveal the man Susan Ann knew saved her life.

"Hi, Miz Carlson, how are you feeling?"

"She's better now, thanks to you," Sam walked up to him and shook his hand.

"I don't know if you remember me. My name is Jeremy Klute. I own my family's farm up on Bodkin Ridge, and I'm a retired mining engineer. I worked for Peason's Mining Company for over sixteen years until the accident. The mine I worked with was about a mile down below where you live. We had a major cave-in eighteen months ago in one of the coal shuts that ended up killing fifteen people, mostly poor kids in their teens just trying to put some food on their families' table. The company tried to hush it up, and a lot of people around here were pointing fingers as to why it happened. It's really been bitter. The tunnels had been shored up properly, but one of the supervisors, Ron Lakeman, pushed the boys to dig and dynamite in places that made the tunnel unstable. He died in that hole, too.

We tried to dig them out. Their families stood by that God-forsaken hole and waited, silent and mournful. They were passed tears. After four days, we didn't hear a sound down there. Then we smelt the gas and knew we had to stop. There was nothing we could do. Walking away, those people looked like they carried Death on their shoulders. Up here, it's a way of life. The generations of harsh living…" He stared off with a look of someone who would never forget. After a moment, he began again.

"We sealed the entrance. We really didn't have a choice. Some of the people came from their homes to watch it being done. In the crowd was your uncle Marvin, Sam, and Granny Pickler. She was pulling at her hair and screaming for her boy, begging them to open the mine, and so she could get him and take him home."

Looking over at Sam, Klute said, "Your uncle Marvin was not known for his patience. He rounded on the old woman, shouting at her to shut up and quit bitchin'. He said Riley was a troublemaker; he was always complaining about his friend Ron. Why, Ron Lakeman was a good man. He went fishing with him about once a week and had more sense than most people around here. That boy of hers probably caused the whole thing."

Looking over at the younger woman in the bed, he said, "That's when people started talking about the curse. Granny Pickler birthed many a fine baby, but she was also known for her spells and cunning ways. A curse brought on by pain and tears is powerful. At first, people in the area whispered; then they waited. They were not surprised that Marvin died the way he did.”

Things were starting to make sense for Susan Ann. She understood now why the men that delivered the gravel acted so funny. Looking over at her family and then back to him, she said,

“So, what really happened to Sam’s uncle Marvin?”

“We’re not really sure, but we think he died the same way you almost did. You have to understand, that when his body was brought to the funeral home, he probably had been out there a day or two before Lemmie found him. By the time he was brought into town, Albert Mock took one look at him and believed he had died of heart failure; and he might have, but it was probably brought on by the gas. We had no doctor in town to run tests or autopsy him, and it was the dog days of summer. Mock prepared him for burial, and the visiting doctor signed the death certificate. Town’s folk knew he was losing it after his wife died. He wouldn’t see anyone or accept help from anybody. We had had a bad drought the year before, and patches of the woodland had dried out. I guess that’s what Marvin though happened to his land in the back.

What he didn’t know was that a good-sized methane pocket had settled into his back lot. The methane was slowly leaking out of the ground and killing everything on the surface that didn’t move, and some that did. It had already killed off his chickens. It was slowly killing him. The leakage had not yet covered the ground around the house proper. That might be the reason he lived so long; I don’t know. By the time the back lot had changed radically, he had not even noticed or cared.

When I heard you, folks had moved onto Marvin’s land. The whispers started again. Not long afterward, I heard about Susan Ann’s visions. Good thing people like to talk. I knew I had to drop by and take a look at that property to make sure you and your kin were not in danger. Methane gas is highly flammable, too. Explosions can happen without warning. Once I looked at the ground, I called the sheriff from the homestead above your place and came back down to knock on your door.

When the last word was spoken, the young writer stared over at the old woman. The silence was deafening. Finally, she spoke again.

"Was Marvin really cursed? According to many, he was. You don't speak badly of the dead. They may hear you. Marvin was a bitter old man who didn't pay attention to the signs or respect the old ways. Who knows? As to what happened to that young family, was it God's will? I don't know that either. All I know is that if Susan Ann had not had her vision, a young girl would have died up on that mountain.

The mining company went to the homestead and cleaned up the gas as soon as it was reported. I was told that the family moved off their homestead a few days after Susan Ann got out of the hospital. No one's had news of them since."

Getting up from her chair, her hand went to her back. "Might stiff. I may have to go to bed soon." The old woman walked towards the sink and put their coffee cups in.

"Look you; it's getting late. The sun is almost down. Driving these mountain roads can be treacherous at night for someone not used to them. Get some rest and I will see you in the morning. Bright and early, now…I'll have coffee and biscuits awaiting and we'll talk about birthing babies."

The young man said his goodbyes and got in his car. As the door shut on the cabin, he couldn't help but wonder if her story was about a true reckoning. Perhaps God in his own way has taught these people a way of life that was just a little above most. For all the harshness, there was joy. For all the death, there was birth. Something keeps these folks here, generation after generation. Perhaps they understand better than most. As he drove off, he couldn't help but think about tomorrow and wondered if he could even sleep.

Mountain Terms Used in the Book

Conjure folk - People that practice Hoodoo or other types of magic

Cunning folk - People that practice folk healing and medicine making

Dragon's Breath - Fog that curls around a mountain

Fella - Fellow

A Fetch and Carry - Assistant

Foxfire - A fungi or mushroom that glows in the dark

A Granny Woman or Granny Witch - Midwife, healer, spiritual leader; some are makers of

charms and spells

Haint - Ghost or spirit

Haint blue - A light sky blue or Carolina blue

Half a mind - Slow in understanding

Healer Man - Cunning man or medicine man

Heap - A lot

Heerd – Heard

Kin - Family

Lighter Knots - A plug of heartwood pine used to start fires

Mite - Maybe

Miz - Mrs.

Neared - Close to

Reckoning - An understanding

Revenuers - A US Treasury agent whose job is to enforce laws to prevent the illegal distillation of

liquor.

Simples - Herbs used for medicine

Sore need - Real need

Spoofin'- Joking

Water Witch or Water Witcher - Dowser

Will-o-wisp - A ghostly atmospheric light that comes and goes

Ya'll - You all.

References

Andrews, Ted. *Animal-Speak: The Spiritual & Magical Powers of Creatures Great & Small.* Llewellyn Worldwide Ltd. St. Paul, Minn. 1993.

Auchmutey, Jim. "United States: The South." *Encyclopedia of Food and Culture*. Ed. Solomon H. Katz. New York: Scribner, 2003. p. 465-469. (Appalachian farming)

Burdick, Lewis Dayton. *Magic and Husbandry, the Folk-Lore of Agriculture: Rites, Ceremonies, Customs, and Beliefs Connected with Pastoral Life and the Cultivation of the with Fruit-Growing, Bees, and Fowls (1905).* Revised: June 1, 2009.

Crissman, James K. *Death and Dying in Central Appalachia.* University of Illinois Press. Champaign, IL. 1994.

Cross, Tom Peete. *Witchcraft in North Carolina.* Andesite Press. August 12, 2015.

Densmore, Frances. *How Indians Use Wild Plants for Food, Medicine and Crafts.* Dover Publications. New York. 1974.

Erbson, Wayne. *Rural Roots of Bluegrass: Songs, Stories and History*. Mel Bay Publications, Inc. 2003.

Grieve, Margaret. *A Modern Herbal, Vol. 1 A-H, Cosmetic and Economic Properties, Cultivation and Folklore of Herbs, Grasses, Fungi, Shrubs and Trees with their Modern Scientific Uses.* Dover Publication, Inc. New York. 6/1/1971.

Grieve, Margaret. *A Modern Herbal, Vol. 2 I-Z, Cosmetic and Economic Properties, Cultivation and Folklore of Herbs, Grasses, Fungi, Shrubs and Trees with their Modern Scientific Uses.* Dover Publication, Inc. New York. 6/1/1971.

Guiley, Rosemary Ellen. *A Lunar Almanac.* Cynthia Parrych Publishing, Inc. 1991.

Hand, Wayland D. *Magical Medicine: The Folkloric Component of Medicine in the Folk Belief, Custom, and Ritual of the Peoples of Europe and America.* University of California Press. Berkeley, Los Angeles, and London.1981.

Headstrom, Richard. *Identifying Animal Tracks.* Dover Publications. 2012.

Henry, James. *The Bushcraft Bible.* Skyhorse Publishing. New York. 2015.

Hewitt, Tim. Kelly Hartigan (Editor). *Appalachian Trail Myths: The Ugalu & Pamola.* Barnes & Noble Press. New York. 2016.

Hohman, John George. *Pow-Wows or Long Lost Friend.* Wildside Press LLC. 2010.

Jones, Richard A. and **Sharon Sweeney-Lynch**. *The Beekeeper's Bible: Bees, Honey, Recipes & Other Home Uses.* Abrams Publishing. 2011.

Keister, Douglas. *Stories in Stone: The Complete Guide to Cemetery Symbolism.* Smith, Gibbs Publisher. 2004.

Kollerstrom, Nick. *Gardening and Planting by the Moon.* W. Foulsham and Company. 2001.

Kravitz, David. *"TRIVIA". Who's Who in Greek and Roman Mythology.* New York: Clarkson N. Potter, Inc. 1975.

Lewis, James R. *The Astrology Book: The Encyclopedia of Heavenly Influences* (2nd ed.) Detroit: Visible Ink Press. 2003.

Lust, John. *The Herb Book.* Bantam Books. NY. 1978.

McLean, Gordon. A Field Guide to Dowsing: How to Practice the Ancient Art Today. The American Society of Dowsers, 1976.

Mooney, James. *Myths of the Cherokee.* Dover Publications. 1996.

Murray, Kenneth. *Footsteps of the Mountain Spirits. Appalachia: Myths, Legends, and Landscapes of the Southern Highlands.* Overmountain Press. 1992.

Picton, Margaret. *The Book of Magical Herbs.* Barrons Educational Series. NY. Quarto Publishing. London. 2000.

Pinckney, Roger. *Blue Roots: African American Folk Magic of the Gullah People.* Llewellyn Worldwide. St. Paul, MN. 2000.

Richmond, Nancy and Misty Murray Walkup. *Appalachian Folklore: Omens, Signs and Superstitions.* Barnes and Noble. 2011.

Rodale's Illustrated Encyclopedia of Herbs. Kowalchik et al. Rodale Press. 1998.

Rosenberg, Neil. *Bluegrass: A History.* University of Illinois Press. 1985.

Selig, Godfrey. *Secrets of the Psalms.* Fort Worth, TX. Doreen Pub. Co.1982.

Stroud, Rick. *The Book of the Moon.* Walker Publishing Company, Inc. New York. 2009.

Thomas, Robert Bailey. *The Old Farmer's Almanac*. Yankee Publishing. Dublin, NH. 2015.

Wigginton, Eliot & *Foxfire Fund Inc. The Foxfire Book: Hog Dressing, Log Cabin Building,
Mountain Crafts and Foods, Planting by the Signs, Snake Lore, Hunting Tales, Faith Healing,
Moonshining, and Other Affairs of Plain Living Paperback*. Anchor Books. New York. 1972.

Wigginton, Eliot & Foxfire Fund Inc. *Foxfire 2*. Anchor Books. New York. 1973.

Waller, Irene. *Weaving*. Coles Publishing. Toronto. 1978.

Worth, Valerie. *Crone's Book of Charms and Spells*. Llewellyn Worldwide. St. Paul, MN. 2002.

Journals

How to Make Soap from Ashes- Modern Homesteading. **Author:** Paul D. Matteoni. Mother Earth News. (Jan-Feb. 1972). Date Accessed October 4, 2018. Published by: Ogden Publications

Sympathetic Magic in the Kentucky Mountains: Some Curious Folk-Survivals. Author: Josiah Henry Combs Source: The Journal of American Folklore, Vol. 27, No. 105 (Jul.- Sept. 1914), pp. 328-330 Published by: American Folklore Society.

Cites

Webster's New World College Dictionary, 4th Edition. Copyright © 2010 by Houghton Mifflin Harcourt.

Ashrafian, Hutan. "Mathematics in Medicine: the 300-Year Legacy of Iatromathematics." *The Lancet*. VOLUME 382, ISSUE 9907, P1780, (11/30, 2013)

Websites (Cited Reference in book)

Tabler, David. "You don't mean to go into Dark Corner, do you?" Appalachian History, 20 September 2016, Date accessed: 11/17/2018, http://www.appalachianhistory.net/2016/09/you-dont-mean-to-go-into-the-dark-corner-do-you.html